Dedicated to the Moon and the Sun, my daughters:

Sofía and Clara.

"Everything we hear is an opinion, not a fact. Everything we see is a perspective, not the truth."

Marcus Aurelius

INDEX

ACKNOWLEDGEMENTS

Thanks to all the protagonists of this story, especially William H. Ray, Antonio Beas and Víctor Martínez for having to put up with all my questions and for becoming involved in the research for the book.

To Cristian Puig, Óscar Clausell and Rubén Puig for their investigation of the accident, which was the starting point for the realization of this book. Without them this project would never have been possible.

To all the people of Hueva.

To José Manuel "Chaska", for all the help provided, without him an important part of this book would not have been completed.

To the journalist Jesús Ramos, for answering all my questions and letting me use his article: "La Noche de los 24 muertos" (The night of the 24 dead) for the realization of this book.

To a good friend of mine, Civil Guard (Spanish police), who sought for information at Pastrana headquarters, Guadalajara province and in the Department of Historical Studies of the Civil Guard, thank you for your time investigating information from the records.

To all the members of Torrejon Air Force Base, who in August 1973, participated in the recovery of the deceased and the remains of the wrecked plane. Especially, to Steven Cansler, who has helped me actively in the investigation.

Thanks to all the medical staff of Torrejon Air Force Base, for saving the life of the only survivor of the accident, First Lt. William Ray. Especially, to Wade Weaver, for the information provided.

Thanks to all the medical staff of Walson Army Hospital at Fort Dix, New Jersey. Especially to Dr. Rolf Lullof, for the information provided.

Special thanks, to Paul Hansen, for sharing all his investigation about the crash of the C-141 aircraft and for always being available to answer all my questions.

Thanks, to Gary Harpster, who helped me in the investigation of the American naval base at Nea Makri in Greece, trying to find the owner of the Navy Diving Officer's pin.

To James Orzech and his wife Liz Rotti, for helping to confirm that Chris L. Katsetos was the owner of the Navy Diving Officer's pin and for finding a relative of one of the passengers, Charles Edward (Chuck) Hyatt.

To Mike Reagan, Director of the NDSTC (Naval Diving and Salvage Training Center) in Panama City, for helping with the Navy Diving Officer's pin.

To the photographer, Shinji Yoshida "GETA-O" (Japan), for letting me use two of his photos of the C-141 aircraft 63-8077.

To all the administrators of websites dedicated to the memory of C-141 Starlifter aircraft, for all the help provided: Woodie Hall, Mike Novack, Ronan Hubert, Hiroe Takafumi and José Manuel "Chaska".

Special thanks, to all the relatives and friends of the deceased, who have collaborated providing data and photographs for biographies.

To all the people, who have given me permission to use their photographs or documents for the realization of this book.

To all, thank you.

ABOUT THE AUTHOR

Gustavo Doménech was born on October 31, 1976 in Valencia, although he lived most of his childhood in Alberic and later, in Alzira.

He completed his elementary education and junior high in the Franciscan school St. Anthony of Padua in Carcaixent and then high school at IALE school in Eliana.

Gustavo studied English for 5 summers in Hastings, England (UK) and Randolph, Virgina (USA) in addition to his mandatory studies in Spain.

Gustavo's previous university courses were completed, at what was then called COU, conducted in a Spanish school in Boston, Massachusetts (USA), while living in the home of an American family.

Gustavo next attended San Pablo CEU University in Moncada, studying law for one year. The next three years, he studied at the University of History and Archaeology of Valencia.

Finally, after a year without studying, working at the family restaurant, Gustavo obtained a Chef Certification after two years of training, completing his practicum in the Mont Sant Restaurant in Xativa. He continued another year with training in pastry in Gandia CDT School, combining it with his work in the family restaurant.

In 1998 Gustavo met, his future wife, Sara, after eight years of dating, they were married in 2008. His first daughter, Sofia, was born in 2014 and a second daughter, Clara, was born in 2016.

In 2004, Gustavo found one of his great passions, Japanese Martial Arts. He studied "Kodenkan Danzan Ryu Jujutsu", one of the most popular Jujutsu styles in the USA. In 2016, he received the Sandan from his instructor, Shihan Craig Kutil from Eureka, California (USA).

In 2013, Gustavo incorporated other styles to his training including "Kyushojutsu" "Kiaijutsu" and "Bujutsu" (Japanese traditional weapons) with Professor Jean Paul Bindel (France), "Wako Ryu Jujutsu" and "Mondo Ryu Heiho" (combat style with Japanese sword) with the master Soshi Claudio Artusi (Italy). In addition to traveling to many countries for training with great teachers, Gustavo organized numerous courses bringing many international instructors to Alberic where he has his school, "Club Jujitsu Alberic - Kodenkan Komori Dojo".

This is the first time Gustavo has written a book of this magnitude, although he has completed several works of translations of martial arts manuals from English into Spanish. He also wrote a manual, in 2014, about schools with "Hakko Ryu Jujutsu" influences and in 2015, began to write a book about the "Mimawari and Shinsengumi" that has been delayed pending the completion of this book, about the Hueva accident in 1973.

PREFACE

My intention in writing this book, has been collecting all possible information about the crash of the US Air Force C-141 Starlifter 63-8077 plane, which crashed in the village of Hueva, Guadalajara province, Spain in 1973. For this, I have relied on the testimony of its protagonists as direct witnesses and all available written sources: ie letters, official documents, newspapers, magazines, books and websites, where they talk about this event.

The structure of the book is organized by two axes, the first, with the crash of the C-141 aircraft with its 25 occupants and the town of Hueva, and the second, with the only survivor, First Lt. William H. Ray and his rescuers Antonio Beas, Víctor Martínez and the citizens of the town of Hueva, who participated in the rescue.

The purpose from the beginning, has been to honor all those killed in the accident so all their names appeared instead of just being numbers in the statistics of an air accident. The only names that were published, were those of the 7 crew from the USAF, however, the list of the names of the 17 passengers was never published in Spain, only some of their names appeared in the "Trenton Times" newspaper in the United States. With the help of William Ray from the United States and Víctor Martínez, José Manuel "Chaska", Zayda Beas and Cristian Puig we have been able to find the names of all the deceased passengers of the crashed plane.

It has been 43 years since the accident happened, so it has been very difficult to find data on the deceased. In this book I have published all the data and documents that I found. Unfortunately, I have not been able to obtain pictures of them all; in some only a photo of his or her grave and in others not even that.

Although I managed to locate and contact some of the families of the deceased passengers and crew, to date very few have answered my emails or my letters. It is still one of the projects of Víctor

Martínez Viana to hold another memorial in honor of all those killed in Hueva, sometime in the near future.

The format used for time is the military 24-hour format, which uses no separation by a colon between the hours and minutes.

PROLOGUE

Víctor Martínez Viana

With great affection and enthusiasm I accept the challenge and honor of writing this prologue for the book written by my good friend Mr. Gustavo Doménech, based on the unfortunate and horrific plane crash, which occurred on St. Augustine night, August 28, 1973, in the calatrava-alcarreña village of Hueva, Guadalajara province in Spain.

I am pleased that Gustavo has decided to write this book about the 1973 aircraft accident in Hueva and that it will also be translated into English. The village of Hueva, will be proud to see its name on this book.

This selfless young author, is to be commended, for deciding to write this book without any thought of monetary gain, but solely to bring the facts of the 1973 Hueva aircraft accident to his readers.

As a witness to events, I verify that the account presented herein are the facts. The book, retells the incident through the eyes of the three protagonists who experienced the incident in all of its human drama. Gustavo researched the incident fully, trying to contact relatives of the twenty-four casualties. He has reviewed and included information from the United States Air Force accident investigation as well as contacting ex US military officials who specialized in aviation mishaps. Gustavo has presented the information with great accuracy (verifying with authentic and reliable sources) as well as great sensitivity for the twenty-four souls who lost their lives. He has included photos of the accident and reviewed every Spanish and American newspaper article that were published in the days following the accident. He has also included photos from the ceremony of October 20, 1973 in which Antonio Beas, Víctor Martínez and the village of Hueva were commended for their actions on the night of August 28, 1973.

Gustavo in this book evokes the emotional impact of the aircraft accident on the lives of Bill, Antonio, Víctor and the inhabitants of Hueva. He also rightly honors those whose lives were cut short on August 28, 1973 and the people that loved them.

My friend Gustavo, you make us remember, after forty-three years, what we went through that tragic night, (at least for me, and I think for the entire population of Hueva) and those events which can never be forgotten. I know that this book will help to inform the world of the heroic behavior of the people of this Village Alcarreña of Guadalajara and their efforts in saving the life of the one survivor and the regret and distress they feel in not being able to save more lives. Gustavo, all the people of Hueva thank you for your efforts in publishing this book, we will not forget you, asking Hueva's patron, the Christ of Faith, to give you good health.

Hueva, August 28, 2016.
VÍCTOR MARTÍNEZ VIANA

PROLOGUE

William (Bill) Ray

In September of 2015, I returned to Spain for a visit, for the first time, in almost 42 years. The main purpose of my trip from the United States, was to visit the good people of the village of Hueva, in Guadalajara Province, and in particular, to meet with Antonio Beas and Víctor Martínez, who had rescued me from the crash site of an aircraft accident and transported me to a hospital in Guadalajara on the night of August 28, 1973. I was at that time serving as a navigator in the US Air Force, flying C-141 cargo planes out of McGuire Air Force Base, New Jersey, and on that night, I would be the only survivor of a C-141 that crashed enroute from Athens, Greece to Torrejon Air Base near Madrid, Spain.

In the United States, the crash did not receive much press coverage, and the cause of the accident was never considered controversial by the US Air Force. But in Spain, rumors persisted for many years, that the United States covered up the true cause of the accident. These rumors were strengthened by the US Air Force's insistence on completing the investigation quickly and without any help from the Spanish authorities. By the morning after the aircraft accident, the crash site was cordoned off from the local Spanish population, until all bodies and major debris were completely removed from the crash area and until the US Air Force investigation was completed.

In 2013, Juan José Benítez, a famous Spanish author, released another book in his very popular series, "Caballo de Troya" (Trojan Horse), entitled "El Día del Relámpago" (The Day of Lightning). In this book, Benítez recounted the crash of the C-141 in Hueva in 1973, and in this novel, which he hints is based on the truth, has the C-141 shot down by an American F-4 in order to conceal the astonishing cargo and intentions of some of the passengers on board. Benítez's book reignited the rumors concerning the 1973 plane crash, and introduced a whole new generation of Spaniards to the controversy surrounding the incident, particularly among his devoted fans.

The first afternoon I arrived in Hueva in September, 2015, I was met by Cristian Puig, Rubén Puig, Óscar Clausell, and Paco Navarrete from Valencia, Spain, who asked if they might interview me concerning the C-141 crash in Hueva in 1973. Their purpose was to find out the truth of the causes of the plane crash and to dispel any unfounded rumors about the accident. We drove to the accident site and I told them all that I could remember. Later I was contacted, via email, by their colleague, Gustavo Doménech, who had become interested in the story, proposed to research the incident further, and to put the results down in written format. Gustavo also became interested in the story from the standpoint of all the passengers and crew whose promising lives had been so tragically cut short. He proposed to contact the family members of the casualties and include in his book the stories of the lives of those who perished in the crash.

What follows is the result of all of Gustavo's labors. Many thanks to Gustavo for all of his hard work on this project. I hope the reader will find Gustavo's work interesting and insightful.

Bill Ray

INVESTIGATION

The idea for the creation of this book, stems from a tragic event which occurred in the town of Hueva (Spain) in 1973, where it all ended for an American military aircraft Lockheed C-141 Starlifter and its occupants. All? No, not all. Out of this terrible event and in this place, will grow a friendship between three people that will remain with them throughout their lives as blood brothers.

I usually help my cousins Cristian Puig and Rubén Puig in their research, writing letters or making translations in English. Since 2014, I was helping Rubén Puig to find out who might be the person hidden inside a diving suit that appeared in a photograph. We tried to solve one of the contests on the website of the famous Spanish writer J.J. Benítez.

In September 2015, my cousins contacted me asking if I could accompany them for the weekend to Hueva, a town near Guadalajara, about a 4 hour drive from where I live. They needed someone who spoke English because they were going to interview the sole survivor of a C-141 plane crash in 1973. Unfortunately, I could not go.

By chance, one day after that trip my cousin Cristian appeared. While we were eating the famous Doménech sandwich, he was telling me how everything had gone with the interview with the sole American survivor, First Lieutenant William Ray. I found the story fascinating. Just when he was finishing telling what happened, he showed me some photographs in which an US Navy Diving Officer's pin with a diver's helmet appeared which had been found at the crash site by one of the inhabitants of Hueva. I do not know why, but when I saw the diver's helmet, I thought it could be related to the other case that we had been investigating since 2014. Soon I would dismiss any connection, but I was so immersed investigating, that I couldn't stop without finding all the answers to the unknown factors surrounding the plane crash.

This book and the research I started in October 2015 cannot be understood, without going back to 2013 and to the research initiated on the Hueva accident by Cristian Puig, Óscar Clausell and Rubén Puig.

On October 12, 2013 after learning about the plane crash through a novel, **Cristian Puig, Óscar Clausell and Rubén Puig** began an investigation, visiting the town of Hueva, Guadalajara province. They wanted to know what had really happened and contrast the information that appeared in the book "El día del relámpago" (The Day of Lightning) from the famous Spanish writer J.J. Benítez. In this novel, it is said that the plane had been shot down by an US F-4 Phantom fighter to eliminate the boss and several executives from "Trojan Horse" top secret project. Following their initial investigation they found many unanswered questions and the case would require a much more thorough investigation.

How could it be otherwise, by chance or as we like to call it, the synchronicity of life, played its role in this story. Just two years later, during a visit to our friends from Hueva, we were told that the only survivor returned to visit them after 42 years since the accident had occurred. Thanks to the kindness of these people and the help of fate, Rubén, Cristian and Óscar could meet with First Lieutenant William Ray and record a series of videos about the accident, including an interview with William Ray narrating the facts of the accident in the place where the plane had crashed.

Watched in retrospective and with all the information gathered since then, maybe these videos were based on mistaken premises that we would discover as the investigation progressed and deepened. However, the creation of these videos would have an unimaginable positive impact for the investigation, being essential for locating in Spain, the list with all the names of the passengers.

As it couldn´t be any other way, I started reading J.J. Benítez´s book: "El día del relámpago" (The Day of Lightning) I wanted to know his version of the accident and if there was any mention of a scuba diver.

I contacted First Lieutenant **William H. Ray** via Facebook on November 3, 2015. He was the only survivor of the accident and a direct witness of the facts. After a few messages and after asking him permission to ask questions about the accident, we continued communicating through his personal email. William became key in clarifying the facts of the accident, helping me actively to obtain documentation and correcting the English version of this book.

On November 4, 2015 I visited several web pages that deal with the crash of the C-141. Among them was a Spanish website **"Hueva.net"** in which a wide section is devoted to the description of the accident, accompanied by numerous photos of the hill where the plane crashed. It would not be until December 18, 2015 when I made contact by phone with the author and administrator of this website, **José Manuel "Chaska"**. The clue to finding, in Spain, the complete list of all the passengers that perished in the crash of the C-141 near Hueva on August 28, 1973, came from my initial conversation with José Manuel.

The next day, I found the report of **Paul Hansen** "http://c141heaven.info/dotcom/mishap_paul_hansen.htm" where all the information concerning C-141 aircraft accidents throughout its history are collected. Most web pages on the Internet use his synopsis to explain the events surrounding the accident. I contacted Paul Hansen via email and it took him only 15 minutes to respond. He devoted himself to help, sending me all newspapers and magazines articles he had on the Hueva accident (Torrejon 1973), plus his updated report, from June 2013, with all C-141 aircraft accidents.

Other websites which have provide valuable information during my research include "C-141 Flying Squadrons" by **Woodie Hall** and "C141 Heaven" by **Mike Novack**. Both pages contain extensive information on the C-141 cargo plane and their crews. Their administrators have always been available to clarify any doubts that arose during the investigation.

Not all research lines have been successful. The Navy Diving Officer´s pin gave me the idea of looking for potential sources at the US base of **Nea Makri** in Greece. On November 7, 2015 I attempted to locate scuba divers at that base, that could remember the accident in Spain and with luck, would remember the name of one of the passengers on the C-141. I found a blog where they were talking about scuba diving instructors who were at that base, however my attempts to contact them were unanswered. The next day I started searching on Facebook and sent messages to several people who were in Nea Makri in 1973. Fifteen days later, on November 23, 2015 **Gary Harpster** replied to me. Although he did not remember the plane crash, he offered his help contacting other colleagues who were also in Nea Makri at that time. Unfortunately no one remembered anything of the accident in Spain. It ended up being a dead end and I ended that line of investigation.

On December 17, 2015 I found on Facebook a post from **Robert Rodriguez** dated August 24, 2013 related to Hueva accident, which led me to locate the group "Torrejon AFB Spain". I published several posts about the accident and thanks to some members of that group, I was able to contact several users who were part of the rescue teams and the medical team that treated William in the Torrejon Air Force Base hospital.

On February 24, 2016 I wrote a letter to the journalist **Jesús Ramos**, author of the article about the accident: "La noche de los 24 muertos" (The night of the 24 dead), published in the newspaper "La Actualidad Española" on September 6, 1973. On March 1, I received his response through an email, in which he allowed me to ask all the questions I wanted about the accident. He confirmed that the photographer, Rogelio Leal, who was with him taking photos of the crash site had died a few years ago. Thanks to his answers and all the information in his article I gained a clearer understanding of the events and the scene of the day after the accident.

On March 23, 2016, thanks to William Ray I was able to make contact with **Steven Cansler**. Steve was a military security police man, who was stationed in the crash site that fateful day of August 29, 1973. Years later, he would relive that event in the form of vivid dreams, which would lead him to return to Hueva in 2000 to try to put an end to this tragic event, that reappeared again after so many years in his life. Steve will help me from the beginning, giving me plenty of information, especially about the work done the day after the accident.

Seven months after I began the investigation, I had already obtained enough information to meet with the Spanish protagonists of this story: Antonio Beas and Víctor Martínez. On April 11 and 12, 2016 I visited Hueva for the first time, accompanied by Cristian Puig to interview them, unfortunately Víctor lives in Madrid and it was not possible to meet him on that trip. I interviewed **Antonio Beas** and visited the crash site. On this visit I also met his wife Josefa and his daughter Zayda. In the bar "Chispa", that they own in Hueva, there is a folder with many newspaper clippings about the accident and they allowed me to scan them all, along with some letters.

After speaking on the telephone with **Víctor Martínez** the day before, I wrote him an email on April 13, 2016 explaining the research I was carrying out in writing the book about the crash of the American military C-141, that occurred near Hueva on August 28, 1973. A week later Víctor sent me an email with his account of the events which occurred, including several photographs. On April 24, we arranged to meet in Madrid on May 14, 2016 for an interview. In this interview, I told Víctor what the main themes of the book would be and how the research had developed and was progressing. Víctor immediately began helping me research everything he could, giving me numerous photographs. He was also instrumental in locating the list of all the names of the casualties on May 2, 2016, in Spain. Later I also located the list in two different places in the United States.

Locating **relatives of the victims** was a task to which I have devoted much time and effort. On May 3, 2016, the same day I received the list of casualties, I began the work of tracking down all the names on the Internet. My search immediately gave me a clue about one of my goals in writing the book, who was the owner of the **Navy Diving Officer's pin**? His name was Chris Katsetos and he studied Ocean Engineering (Phd in Oceanic Engineer). The first reference appeared in the book: "Blue & Gold and Black: Integration of the US Naval Academy" by Robert J. Schneller in 2008. In this book, Chris Katsetos appears with two friends, James Orzech and Emerson Carr. A second reference, appeared written by one of the cousins of Chris Katsetos, Dr. Christos Katsetos. After several unsuccessful attempts to contact his cousin, I decided to send a letter to James Orzech.

I continued my research but did not receive any response from James Orzech, so I decided to open another line of investigation. On May 17, 2016, I contacted the **NDSTC** (Naval Diving Salvage Training Center) school in Panama City, Florida to see if they could tell me what rank a diving officer had to be. Then I could determine which of the seven possible passengers owned the Navy Diving Officer's pin. I also contacted another base linked to the NDSTC the "Naval Support Activity Panama". On May 23, the NDSTC center's director, Mike Reagan, answered me stating that the minimum rank for a diving officer in 1973 would be "Ensign" or "Lieutenant Junior Grade" (rank O-1 or O-2). The rank to be a Navy diving officer could include all officer ranks. Therefore, none of the passengers who were officers in the Navy could be ruled out.

On June 3, 2016 I received an email from **James Orzech** answering my letter. He confirmed that the passenger Chris Katsetos was his best friend and both were official licensed divers in 1968 at the United States Naval Academy in Annapolis, Maryland. One of the questions of my research was resolved, where had the US Navy Diving Officer´s pin which had been found at the crash site come from? In addition, thanks to a friend of his, Liz Crotty, I could contact with the brother of one of the passengers called "Hyatt", who sent me a newspaper clipping from 1973, in which a photo of his brother appears along with a short biography.

After several months and many attempts trying to locate relatives or friends of all the victims of the accident, I've only received positive responses from relatives or friends of nine of them: Edward Anthony Fanelli, Austin Frederick Balkman, Donald Lee Rhodes, Charles Edward Hyatt, Janice Lynn Barron, Michael Merricks, Chris Louis Katsetos, Clinton Clifford Corbin and Friedrich Hugo Lamers.

To conclude this brief introduction to my twelve months of research, I will answer a question that has continually been made to me throughout my research: why are you trying to find all this information about the accident? It's a good question. My family has asked me that question many times and the answer at first was: For no particular reason. Later, I realized I had many reasons to complete the story that surrounded the accident once and for all, and especially one that I could not explain and it was always pointing me in the right direction, bringing together many people throughout this adventure. There is a shorter and simple answer: Because no one else had done, or was doing a complete account of the accident, in the 43 years that have passed since it occurred.

THE AIRCRAFT

C-141A 63-8077
Yokota AFB June 3, 1972
Courtesy of GETA-O

The history of military airlift includes endless and constant search for larger, more advanced, and increasingly more capable aircraft systems. In 1973, the Lockheed C-141 Starlifter was the workhorse of transport aircraft from the United States Air Force.

In 1956, MATS (Military Air Transport Service) was criticized for the use of C-118 Liftmaster and C-121 Super Constellation aircraft, for being militarized versions of civilian aircraft, that simply, had not been designed to accommodate the Army's air transport requirements. What was needed, was a large modern aircraft, designed solely for military use, capable of transporting the Army's troops and heavy equipment together, thereby ensuring the timely transportation and delivery of more efficient fighting forces.

C-141A 63-8077
Yokota AFB March 13, 1967
Courtesy of GETA-O

The Air Force needed to maintain a strong transport force that could provide a much quicker response capability.

The most important action to come out of the Air Force's 1958 modernization plan, was the decision to begin developing, from scratch, a cargo jet to be operationalized in the 1966-70 time frame. This aircraft became the C-141 Starlifter, for its time, the most significant transport aircraft brought into the USAF (United States Air Force) inventory. Later, it would be replaced a few at a time, by the C-5 Galaxy. The C-141 was known as the "Starlifter" a name that came from an employee, after Lockheed conducted an in-house contest to name the new aircraft.

As an indication of the significance of the need for an improved military transport aircraft, President Kennedy himself announced the Lockheed as the winner of the design competition for its "Super Hercules" in March 1961. More than two years later, in August 1963, the first C-141 rolled out of the Lookheed factory in Georgia, and on December 17, 1963 made its maiden flight. The last of 284 aircraft was delivered December 1968.

Maiden flight December 17, 1963

One Lockheed C-141A-LM Starlifter Construction Number 300-6110 did not receive a USAF serial number, was flown with civil registration N4141A and later as NASA N714NA. The aircraft began as a Lockheed Model L-300 Starlifter jet transport, originally configured as a prototype commercial version of the US Air Force C-141A. The airplane was modified to house the Kuiper Airborne Observatory (KAO) telescope for use at very high altitudes. Operated between 1966 and 1995, this NASA NC-141A is now in storage at NASA Ames Research Center, Moffet Federal Airfield, California.

NASA NC-141A at Ames Research Center

The C-141 Starlifter was procured under the novel "concurrent acquisition and test" concept rather than following a standard practice of developing a prototype aircraft for test and evaluation. Under this philosophy, the C-141 entered the operational force prior to the completion of the Category II Test Program. The rationale behind the concurrent concept was to have a weapon system become productive sooner. MATS received the C-141 at least two to three years earlier under this method and then later awarded a series of modification projects to correct deficiencies.

The production timeline was 4 aircraft in 1963, 8 aircrafts in 1964, 56 aircrafts in 1965, 106 aircrafts in 1966, 107 in 1967 and 4 aircrafts in 1968.

The C-141 primary mission was to move material around the world, from one air base to another. The cargo that they flew ranged from everything from engines, building materials, caskets with the remains of deceased military personnel, to the US Mail. Just about anything and everything that you could imagine that had a high priority, the Air Force flew on C-141s.

Once they knew how much material they had to load on the plane, then they would allow passengers, as long as there was space available.

Military personnel with orders got the highest priority for an available seat.

Wives and immediate family members (the children) of military personnel with orders also got a high priority for a seat.

Military personnel without orders who were on leave (on vacation) were entitled to a seat, if space was available.

Retired military personnel were also entitled to a seat if space was available.

In late 1979 the USAF discovered that the volume of the cargo was relatively small compared to the loading capacity. It ran out of physical space before reaching its maximum transport weight limit. The 270 C-141A models were elongated with additional fuselage sections added in front and behind the wings, lengthening the fuselage 7.11 meters. This modification, which resulted in the B configuration, also added the in-flight refueling capability.

Assembly line at Lockheed factory for configuration B

In 1994, 13 C-141B's were modified to SOLL II level (Special Operations Low-Level II), which provided the aircraft the ability to fly at low altitude at night and improved defensive measures.

In 1997, approximately 60 "B" model aircraft were further upgraded to a "C" model configuration, with improved avionics, navigation systems and incorporating a "glass cockpit".

Models C-141 A and B

Several other upgrades had significant impact on the aircraft operational mishap experience. The chart below highlights some of the more important equipment upgrades.

SUMMARY OF MAJOR MODIFICATIONS	
Equipment	Year of Introduction
Add AN/APN 169B Station-Keeping Equipment	1975
Upgrade Pressure Door	1976
Add INS	1977
Add Ground Proximity Warning System (GPWS)	1978
Upgrade Cargo Ramp Locking Mechanism	1978
Modify to "B" Configuration	1979
Modify Braking System	1979
Remove Auto Spoilers	1980 (?)
Replace APN-59 Radar with Bendix Color Radar	1981
Cockpit Voice Recorder and improved Flight Recorder	1983
Add Fuel Savings Advisory System (FSAS)	1983
Glass Cockpit for selected "C" model aircraft	1997
Add Traffic Collision Alert System (TCAS)	1999

The C-141 had made a quantum leap forward by obviating many of the historic airlift limitations. Nine overlapping limitations on airlift technology are identify: speed, range/payload trade-offs, flexibility of employment in a wide array of scenarios, cubic capacity, load ability, aircraft self-sufficiency, fuel efficiency, direct operating costs, and terminal base requirements. No single aircraft had ever overcome all of these difficulties, and probably one never will.

Analysis of C-141 total hull loss accidents conducted by Lt. Col. Paul Hansen (USAFR, Ret. of McChord Air Force Base, WA) on June 1, 2013 revealed that the most common cause of C-141 accidents would have been human error, in other words, human factors causing more than 70% of total hull loss accidents.

The most common hull-loss mishap was caused by Controlled Flight into Terrain (CFIT). With the introduction in 1978 of a Ground Proximity Warning System (GPWS), the rate of mishaps was reduced dramatically. Fatigue was a constant hazard of the strategic airlift missions, with long duty days and multiple time zones, with nearly 50% of the mishaps occurring at night.

Air traffic control was also a factor in operational hull-loss mishaps, with two mishaps for confusion over an ATC clearance that directly led to the mishap.

In Hueva Spain accident, all these factors came together to form a chain of events that led to the tragic outcome. The plane that crashed in Hueva, a Lockheed C-141A-10-LM Starlifter with identification number 63-8077 / 300-6008, was the eighth that came out of the Lockheed-Georgia Co. factory in Marietta in 1964, along with the sixth and seventh which were intended for the USAF testing programs.

Lockheed C-141A-10-LM with identification number 63-8077

The remarkable 43 year career of the C-141 Starlifter came to an end, with the last flight of aircraft 66-0177, known as "Hanoi Taxi", in May 2006. The ability to airlift large loads over intercontinental distances in a matter of hours was the result of a revolution in airlift capability and responsiveness.

As a curiosity, it is interesting that the C-141 aircraft that crashed in Hueva or at least its identification number was possibly one of the best known in the US Air Force. The plane number 38077 was used as a model, for many years, for the manufacture of a plastic kit by Aurora Models Company.

C-141A 38077 model produced by Aurora Models Company

LOCKHEED C-141 STARLIFTER		
Official **Designation**	**C-141A** **Model**	**C-141B** **Model**	**C-141C** **Model**
Primary Role	Strategic airlift		
Secondary Role	Special operations and aeromedical evac		
National Origin	United States of America		
Contractor	Lockheed-Georgia Co.		
Operator	United States Air Force and NASA		
Wingspan	160 feet (48.77m)		
Length	44.2m	168 feet, 4 inches (51.3m)	
Height at Tail	39 feet, 7 inches (12.07m)		
Wing Surface	300m²		
Cargo Hold	Length: 104 feet, 3 inches (31.76m) Width: 10 feet, 3 inches (3.11m) Height: 9 feet (2.74m)		
Armament	None		
Engines	4 Pratt & Whitney TF33-P-7 turbofans		
Thrust	21,000 pounds (94kN) per engine		
Cruise Speed	520 mph (837km/h; Mach 0.70)		
Max Speed	571 mph (919km/h)	566 mph (912km/h)	
Range	5,550 nm (10,279km) without cargo; Unlimited as from models "B" with inflight refueling.		
Service Ceiling	41,600 feet (12,680m)		
Operating Weight	144,492 pounds (65,540kg)		
Fuel	JP-4 (50% Kerosene 50% Gasoline) With corrosion and icing inhibitors and antistatic agent.		
Fuel Capacity	153,532 pounds (25,139 gallons or 95,162 liters)		
Max Payload	70,850 pounds (32,135kg)	90,880 pounds (41,220kg)	

Pallets	10	13	
Crew	From 5 (pilot, co-pilot, navigator, engineer and load master) to 8 (2 pilots, co-pilot, 2 navigators, 2 engineers and a load master). Medical evacuation missions had two nurses and three doctors.		
Passengers	154 troops 123 paratroops	205 troops 168 paratroops	
Date First Flight	December 17, 1963	March 24, 1977	
Date Deployed	October 1964	December 1979	October 1997
Retirement	May 6, 2006		
Production	1963 - 1968		
Total Produced	285: 284 USAF / 1 NASA		

FLIGHT ROUTE

Z Sunday, 26 Aug 73	Local	McGuire		Action
1400	1000	1000		Awake (estimate)
1615	1215	1215		Alert
1915	1515	1515		Depart McGuire
Monday, 27 Aug 73				
0315	0415	2315	(26 Aug)	Arrive Torrejon
0745	0845	0345		Depart Torrejon
1225	1425	0825		Arrive Classified Location
1325	1525	0925		Depart Classified Location
1520	1720	1120		Arrive Athens
1800	2000	1400		Night in Athens
2200	2400	1800		Bed
Tuesday, 28 Aug 73				
0500	0700	0100		Awake
0530	0730	0130		Breakfast
0700	0900	0300		Tour Athens
1200	1400	0800		Lunch
1415	1615	1015		Alert
1820	2020	1420		Depart Athens
2145	2245	1745		Crash

Cronological account of activities of previous
72 hours before the accident

Some days before the fateful flight of the C-141A 63-8077 that would end in Hueva, First Lt. William H. (Bill) Ray, navigator, received orders to join this mission to replace one of the navigators originally assigned who had become ill.

The night of the Saturday, August 25, 1973, William and his wife had dinner with friends. Soon afterwards, he began to feel unwell. Bill called the navigator scheduler of the 18 MAS at McGuire AFB in New Jersey, and asked for a replacement because he was feeling so ill. The scheluder told him he would try to find another navigator to take the flight, but could not find anyone at that late time. The scheduler proposed to him, since this mission had two navigators, arranging the over-water navigation responsibility with the second navigator on the mission, Major Lamers, so Bill would have responsibility for the return over water portion of the journey rather than the first over-water leg. Bill agreed this would be an acceptable solution and remained on the mission.

In retrospect, Bill has often had the feeling that fate was determined to keep him off this flight, and finally to put him in the only seat on the plane in which someone survived. It is curious, although Bill did not have any comprehension of it, fate also pulled the strings the night of Tuesday August 28, 1973, such that both Antonio Beas and Víctor Martínez would be in Hueva and could perform the feat of saving his life. From a rational point of view, Bill knows he only survived through a combination of lucky circumstances and the assistance of the good people of Hueva.

McGuire Air Force Base, New Jersey

At 1215 they received the routine call "alert" and went to the base, arriving in the squadron office dressed in flight suit uniform with a bag packed with uniforms and civilian clothes, in addition to their specific equipment and the checklists for C-141. At base operations they received the flight route with the weather report. Then they were taken to the plane where they loaded their belongings and performed the physical inspection of the plane. The navigator was required to calculate the amount of fuel required for the flight based on the weight of the aircraft, the cargo and the duration of the flight and to verify his calculations with the amount of fuel actually placed in the fuel tanks.

The crew once in the cabin performed their duties of ensuring that all the equipment was operating properly. Every crew member went through their respective checklists before take-off. Once all preflight requirements were completed the flight would be cleared for takeoff on August 26, 1973 at 1515 from McGuire Air Force Base with a destination of Beirut in Lebanon, with one stop for refueling at the Torrejon de Ardoz Air Base in Spain.

C-141 landing at Torrejon Air Force Base in 1973, Spain
Photo courtesy of Jim Smith

It was a routine flight, this first leg of the mission over the Atlantic, with Major Lamers performing the navigator duties. They arrived at Torrejon Air Base at approximately 0315 (Spanish local time) where they stopped for about 2 hours to refuel and continue their way to Beirut, that was the destination of the cargo they carried. They left Torrejon smoothly, with First Lt. Ray on duty as the navigator until the arrival in Athens. They continued the next leg of the mission, an approximately 6 hour flight, and arrived at 1425 (local time) at Beirut International Airport. All the cargo would be unloaded there, and one hour later, at 1525 they took off heading for Athens, Greece, where they would crew-rest for 24 hours.

Beirut Airport 1973, Lebanon

Hellenikon Air Base

After a short two-hour flight they landed around 1720 (local time) at Hellenikon Air Base (Ellenikon International Airport closed since 2001). After being on duty for 22 hours since their departure from McGuire AFB, the crew was extremely tired. US Air Force regulations required a 24 hour crew rest after this length of flying duty. The crew was anxious to see the sights of Athens. They ate dinner and then went to see the sound and light show from the base of the Acropolis; spotlights illuminating the ancient structures while a voice was describing each of the buildings, ending with traditional Greek music. The view of those structures from the terrace where they were was almost magical. They returned to their hotel and slept.

The next morning, before their next crew duty day would begin, the crew did some sightseeing in Athens and visited a museum. Tuesday August 28, 1973 they were alerted 24 hours after their crew-rest had begun in Athens. This time their C-141 would transport some passengers returning to the United States and a lesser amount of cargo, according to the official investigation report, 5896 kg (13,000 lbs) spread over 3 pallets and according to the newspapers at the time, approximately 9000 kg (19,841 lbs). After ensuring all the security checks, they were allowed to take off around 2020 (local time) heading Torrejon Air Base, where they would make a stop to refuel and would head home, to complete the last leg of the mission at McGuire Air Force Base.

THE ACCIDENT AUGUST 28 1973

It was 2020 when the aircraft —mission number SAAM 1938— took off from Athens Airport. The plane slid silently through the cold air and soon reached the assigned altitude. The crew not on duty retired to rest in the bunks. Everything was quiet, they saw the snowy mountains, the islands, the lighted ships, a delusion for what awaited the crew.

Descent and landing would be made in the dark of night but using VFR (Visual Flight Rules) rather than using IFR (Instrument Flight Rules). The Torrejon weather report was favorable with clear skies and visibility of 10 nautical miles (18.5 km). The moon dipped below the horizon at 2044 and with it the illumination which might have altered subsequent events.

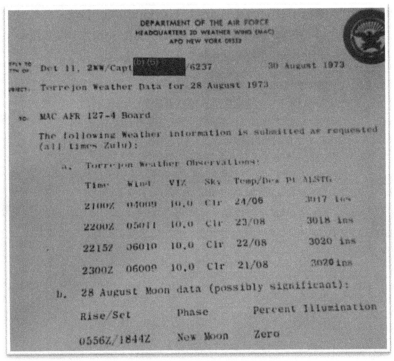

Torrejon Weather information

The C-141 M38077 was en route entering Spain via Valencia and Castejon maintaining altitude FL 330 (33000 feet or 10058.4 meters). At 2225 the aircraft was authorized to descend to FL 100 (10,000 feet or 3048 meters) and ten minutes later to FL 60 (6000 feet or 1828.8 meters). At 2240 it was authorized to descend along the route to Torrejon radio beacon maintaining 5000 feet (1524 meters), but due to the crews misunderstanding of the communications, they began a descent to 3000 feet. At 2245 the aircraft crashed into a hill near the town of Hueva, altitude 3050 feet (929.64 meters) at a speed of 217.5 knots (402.81 km / h).

The plane had disappeared from radar and Torrejon GCA began contacting Madrid Approach Control to check if they had contact with the C-141 and sent several messages expecting to receive a positive response: "M38077 this is Torrejon GCA, how do you hear?... M077, this is Torrejon CGA, if you hear me ident", but no one answered back. One of the F-4 fighters that were conducting maneuvers reported seeing a flash in the descent area of the C-141 so CGA authorized one of the fighters to fly over that area. A few minutes later the fighter confirmed that the plane had crashed into a hill and Torrejon AFB initiated an alert to organize rescue groups.

The plane continued to skid along the ground while it was breaking apart to the point that the cabin was completely separated from the remainder of the aircraft. This main portion of the fuselage was launched into the air and fell again inverted into the ground. The fuel cargo produced several explosions creating a shock wave that shattered the windows of some houses in Hueva and simultaneously lit up the night, to the point that for Hueva residents it looked like the night had become day.

Going back to the moments before the accident, the crew members in the cabin did not notice anything out of the ordinary; everything was like any other descent except for some radio interferences. First Lt. William Ray, the navigator who was not on duty, was trying to sleep in the OACM (Outboard Additional Crew

Member) seat in the cabin just behind the navigator who was on duty, Major Friedrich Lamers. At the beginning of the descent First Lt. Ray put on his headset and connected them just to hear the last three radio communications. In the first one, the controller was giving their distance from Torrejon TACAN (Tactical Air Navigation System, used by military aircraft that provides the user with information about bearing and distance to a ground station or ship-borne station). In the second, Major Lamers warned the pilots that they were at an altitude too low for local geography. In the third one, the pilot looked ahead and said everything seemed fine. A few seconds later the impact would occur.

First Lieutenant William Ray felt the horrible initial impact against the ground and remembers well how various objects hurtled forward by the sudden deceleration, among them an oxygen bottle and an emergency axe. He also remembers the noise that was made by the metal from the cabin that was slowly cracking while they were sliding down the hill at full speed. Shortly after, he was thrown clear out of the cabin and it was from this miraculous serendipity of circumstances that he would become the sole survivor of this tragedy.

The mathematical odds against Bill for not being another one in the list of the deceased were overwhelming. Taking into consideration the aircraft impact against the ground, the deceleration forces, the friction forces of the aircraft with the ground, being thrown out from the aircraft cabin, falling into a place without being struck by any piece of the plane, falling into a place free of fire in the midst of that sea of gasoline and kerosene, that none of the explosions affected him, the truth is that it is something inexplicable that Bill survived when you see the state in which the aircraft remained after the impact. This was noted in the report of the official USAF investigation, stressing that there was no adequate explanation on a scientific basis to explain how the sole survivor could survive, marking in the report the cause for the survival of the First Lieutenant William Ray as "luck".

17.	FACTOR THAT HELPED RESCUE/RECOVERY
	1-RESCUE PERSONNEL TRAINING
	2-TRAINING OF PERSON TO BE RESCUED
	3-AIRCRAFT EMERGENCY ESCAPE MEANS
	4-PERSONAL EQUIPMENT RELEASES/ACTUATORS
	5-RESCUE PROCEDURES/PRE-ACCIDENT PLANS
	6-AVAILABILITY OF RESCUE EQUIPMENT
	7-SUITABILITY OF RESCUE EQUIPMENT
	8-SURVIVOR'S TECHNIQUES
	9-COORDINATION OF RESCUE EFFORTS
X	10. Luck

"Luck", factor for the survival of
First Lieutenant William Ray according to USAF

William had the feeling of tumbling through the air. When he awoke the plane had disintegrated and he was somewhat dazed. Soon his mind began to process everything that had happened, they had had an accident, they had crashed somewhere near Torrejon airport and all he could see around him was fire everywhere. He had to get away from there as far as possible until the emergency services arrived. He removed some cables that had wrapped around his legs and unfastened the belt that kept him attached to the seat, trying to stand up he collapsed on the ground and the feeling of pain in his legs began to increase. The pain was becoming unbearable but he had to leave there no matter what. It seemed to him that nearby was an area that had burned already so he crawled to that area and there he remained enduring the pain wondering if he'd be lucky and someone would come to rescue him before it was too late.

First Lieutenant William Ray´s seat found
in the left side of the cockpit wreckage

On August 28, 1973 what William did not lack was luck. Soon between the flames he thought he saw the silhouette of a person running from one place to another. He could hear that the silhouette was shouting but could not understand what he was saying, so William thought it must be a Spanish citizen. Unfortunately, William did not remember the word for help in Spanish and the only word that came to mind in Spanish was "please" and so he shouted: "POR FAVOR!". Antonio Beas lunged at him and tried to help him to stand up but it was impossible, so Antonio picked him up and took him about fifteen meters away calling to his brother in law Víctor Martínez to help him. Between both of them they took him out of the fire area and with the help of other persons from Hueva who had also got to the crash site they got him into Antonio´s car and they took him away at full speed toward Guadalajara.

Events of the rescue after the accident cannot be understood without going back to the time of the impact of the plane against the hill and how the shock wave from the blast startled all the villagers of Hueva. Antonio Beas and Víctor Martínez were with their families at the home of their in-laws and from the window they could see a great glow in the area of the Serranos. Everyone was in the streets so they decided to take Antonio's car a Seat 124D and headed to that area to see if anyone needed help. Before getting into the car Víctor told a neighbor to warn the mayor of Hueva, Federico Plaza Aguirre, to immediately contact the civil government of Guadalajara to request they send help as soon as possible.

Antonio and Víctor were the first ones to reach to the crash site. There were two separate areas on fire, so they decided to separate to see if they could find any survivors. Víctor took a few turns around his area checking everything that was burning, he thought it was impossible that anyone had survived this disaster and after a small explosion he decided to go back to the area where his brother-in-law was. Antonio reached the area where the cabin of the airplane appeared to be. As he got closer he could glimpse in more detail its size. It was huge. It would be impossible without a ladder to get up there to see if there was any survivor. He shouted to see if someone answered and bordering the cabin he could see someone on the ground with his arm raised. His heart quickened and he immediately pounced on the survivor.

The survivor was conscious, wearing an Air Force flight suit and was talking to him, but Antonio did not understand what he was saying, so he picked him up and dragged him out a few meters away from the fire area. Víctor arrived soon and Antonio tried to pass the survivor to him and go back to see if he could find someone else, but William had grabbed Antonio's neck so strong that the three of them fell down. Antonio and Víctor decided to take him out to the area where the other people who came up from the village were waiting, Milagros Serrano, Isidro Sánchez Saez, Federico Plaza Aguirre and "Quico" Francisco Jimenez Sanchez, who gradually joined them and helped them carry the survivor until they put the survivor in the back of Antonio´s car.

Antonio was driving at full speed and Víctor was in the back holding, as best he could, William´s legs that were losing quite a lot of blood. Víctor alternately told Antonio: "Speed it up or we will lose him and he will die" to "Antonio calm down or you will kill us all." On their way to Guadalajara, they passed by Horche and stopped at the doctor´s house but when the doctor saw the condition in which the wounded was, he told them that he could do nothing and to continue to the hospital in Guadalajara.

Upon reaching the Guadalajara Health Residence of Social Security they placed First Lt. Ray on a stretcher where they cut his flight suit pants legs, cleaned the wounds and put a splint on his broken left leg. After a while a military ambulance arrived to transfer him to the military hospital at Torrejon Air base. The hospital had been advised of the accident and was awaiting the arrival of the survivor. The initial evaluation showed that the patient had multiple abrasions, periorbital ecchymosis (bruising around the eye) and orthopedic injuries in both lower limbs. The medical team struggled to stabilize him because of low blood pressure. The medical team was concerned because the blood loss continued and they couldn´t determine from where the blood loss was taking place. He was taken to the x-rays to check for possible internal injuries and fractures. When they were lifting the left leg for positioning it in the x-ray machine they got the answer, as blood began to pour out from the splint the first responders had placed on the leg in the hospital in Guadalajara. Immediately the splint was removed and the problem of blood loss was solved. It was necessary to begin a transfusion of four units of blood to stabilize him and then he was moved to observation in the intensive care facilities.

The patient was transferred to Frankfurt (Germany) on August 31, 1973, in the "Nightingale" as they called the medical evac aircraft, and from there to Walson Army Hospital at Fort Dix, New

Jersey, arriving on September 2, 1973. William Ray would continue his treatment with Dr. Rolf Lullof in the United States until June 1974 with several operations on his left leg until he received a medical retirement from the US Air Force on July 31, 1974.

Antonio left the car watching as the hospital attendants carried First Lt. Ray into the hospital in Guadalajara. He began to calm down thinking "mission accomplished" and then suddenly all the adrenaline and the stress caused by the rescue weakened him and Antonio collapsed right there. Hospital employees carried Antonio into the hospital on a stretcher and left him in a hallway. Soon after a priest approached and seeing that he was all bloodstained and blackened by smoke from the fire of the crash site mistook him for the person who had been rescued and began to give him the extreme unction. Víctor came quickly and explained to the priest that Antonio was not the wounded they had brought.

The doctor gave Antonio a few tranquilizers and about two hours later they let him go with the condition that Víctor drove back to Hueva. Víctor had had a car accident a week earlier in Tendilla and it was hard for him to drive, but in fits and starts they managed to get to Hueva. Upon arrival the Civil Guard (Spanish Police) had cut all access to the town and they would not let them pass. Víctor explained that they had taken one wounded person from the accident to the hospital in Guadalajara and finally they allowed them to pass. Víctor left his brother-in-law Antonio sleeping at home and then returned to the crash site.

Meanwhile back in New Jersey, Bill's wife, Lilia, was awakened in the middle of the night by loud pounding on her front door. She was used to her husband being away from home for many days at a time with his navigator duties in the Air Force. Her sleep was often interrupted caring for 2 1/2 year old and 11 month old sons, but not by pounding on the front door. She was still half asleep when she answered the door, but her heart came to her throat and she was immediately wide awake when she saw a military chaplain and another Air Force officer standing on her front porch. She knew what that meant. The officers told her that her husband's plane had crashed and that he had survived but that they did not know how badly he had been hurt. They did not have any information on any other survivors. Later in the day, on August 29, she would learn that her husband would live the extent of his injuries, and that everyone else on the flight had perished. The news received at the front doors of 24 other families that day would be much more horrific and life-altering.

Antonio Beas, Víctor Martínez and Juanito with the Seat 124D the day they went to visit William Ray to the military hospital at Torrejon Air Force Base

Neither Antonio Beas or Víctor Martínez have ever seen themselves as heroes for what they did, they always think they could have done much more, that more people could have been saved. It always seems easier when you look back in time and one thinks about everything that could have been done and was not. In my opinion, I think it is demanding too much of themselves and of all the people of Hueva. These people found a hell on earth and had no qualms about risking their own lives to try to find any survivors and rendering assistance selflessly.

Two days later, Antonio, Víctor and their brother-in-law Juanito went to visit William in the hospital at the military base of Torrejon with the Seat 124D. There they could speak very little with him since William was quite sedated and it would not be until his return on October 20, 1973 when William stayed with them a couple days that they got to know each other a little better.

Although for several years they maintained contact through letters and in more recent years by Facebook, it was not until September 2015 when William returned to Hueva, 42 years after being born again, that he would be reunited with Antonio Beas and Víctor Martínez. It was thanks to this visit and to the videos recorded by Cristian Puig, Óscar Clausell and Rubén Puig in which William was explaining how the accident happened and his subsequent rescue, that the idea of writing a book about this entire story will be born in me.

Reencounter 42 years after the accident

DISASTER RECOVERY

Shortly after the F-4 fighter confirmed that the plane had crashed near Hueva, Torrejon Air Force Base was put on alert. The Disaster Preparedness Unit organized a group of first responders from different units to go to the crash site. Among them were firefighters, a medical team, motor vehicle operators, base law enforcement and flight line security police, also known as base security police. The group of security police and base law enforcement was formed by single individuals that were roused from the barracks around 2330. They were living on base so they were the easiest to locate when there was an emergency.

Around 0230 the first group of American rescue teams arrived at the accident site. The Civil Guard (Spanish police) from the nearest towns and several ambulances of the Red Cross from Guadalajara were already there. Firefighters quickly started to work to control the fire of the wreckage, which had spread over several hectares incinerating everything in its path. A small group set up a command post with a radio station, while the other staff had been trying to see if they could find any survivors. The security police team was responsible for keeping people other than the American military personnel away from the crash site.

About 0900 in the morning a bus arrived carrying a second larger group of US military. They were just told that a C-141 had crashed about an hour away from the base with 25 people on board and there was only one survivor. The bus driver drove them as close as he could to the crash site and then they continued on foot to where they thought the command post was. For some reason they assumed that most of the aircraft would still be intact, but when they got to the crash site they found out that the aircraft had been blown to smithereens. With the exception of the cabin, engines, landing gear and the tail of the aircraft, the rest had been reduced to a million tiny and unrecognizable pieces.

With the new reinforcements a perimeter was established with military police placed at intervals of 40 or 50 yards (36.57 or 45.72 meters) around the debris field. Their mission was to initiate recovery operations in their sector, pointing out where the bodies were so the Disaster Preparedness Unit could place them in body bags as they worked their way to each military policeman's position. They also prevented photographers from the press from taking photographs of the bodies.

At 1000 an F-4 fighter made several low passes over the hill taking pictures of the entire area of the accident.

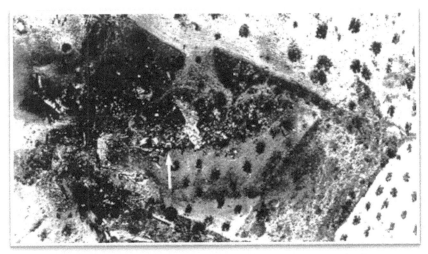

Aerial photo taken by an F-4 with the arrow pointing
to the tail of the C-141

General Salvador Saelices USAF, Torrejon Air Base

About two hours later, the general from the base arrived in a helicopter who was accompanied by two of his aides. The Air Force General Salvador Saelices, remained at the crash site about 45 minutes. He went to the command post to receive first-hand information about what had happened and after a couple of laps around the debris field, observing what was left of the plane, departed again in the same helicopter.

By mid-afternoon, K-rations (combat rations) were distributed, although nobody could really eat anything standing in a field surrounded by human remains and body parts everywhere. While the Disaster Preparedness Unit was responsible for the recovery of the bodies, the rest of the recovery team was recovering documents, mail and money that were just blowing around the crash site during most of the day. A captain was commissioned to accompany the press to assure that only photographs of the charred remains of the aircraft were taken, with strict orders to not allow the press to photograph the bodies.

Once the bodies of all the deceased passengers and crew members were located, they proceeded with the removal of the bodies. The bodies were then transported in a refrigerated truck to the morgue of the military base where autopsies were performed.

After the human remains had been removed, the military investigators could inspect the wreckage in search of the black box, flight instruments, and other flight data recorders. It took them one day to recover all the bodies; however, the recovering of all the bits and pieces of the aircraft would take them two weeks, in which they maintained the presence of the security police 24 hours a day, until the debris field was totally cleared.

Navigator's panel

Some people from the rescue teams stayed on the scene of the accident about 10 to 12 hours before they were relieved from duty. The Air Force didn't have any counselors or therapists waiting for them back at the base. They were expected to shake it off and get back to work. The rescue teams had to put what they had seen out of their minds the best they could and never think about it again.

That morning of August 29, 1973 Víctor Martínez left his brother-in-law at home and went back to the crash site. Upon arrival he was told that the plane that had crashed was carrying 17 passengers and 8 crew and that only one member of the crew had survived, First Lieutenant William Ray. Víctor inquired about the condition of the survivor and was told that he was under observation at the hospital at the military base of Torrejon and was out of danger.

The security police did not let anyone get through the security perimeter and it was not until a Sergeant of the Guardia Civil (Spanish Police) of Pastrana intervened saying: "But he is one of the men that saved the only survivor!" Only then he was authorized to enter the crash site.

Upon reaching the area where the plane had crashed Víctor's heart clenched. With the morning light one could appreciate the magnitude of the catastrophe, nothing to do with the scope of what he remembered of his nocturnal experience. All the land around the crash site had been devastated by fire. The smell in the air was very strong; the pungent smell of fuel intertwined with another odor that he would never forget, the stench of death of the charred bodies. You could clearly see the path the aircraft had followed after the first impact by the holes and the furrows that had been left among the olive groves. Many of the olive trees had their upper branches sheared off and ground up forming a semicircular pattern where the turbines of the engines of the C-141 had chewed through them.

There was virtually nothing left recognizable of the aircraft structure. If Víctor had not been told that a plane had crashed he would have thought that a bomb had exploded there. It was a Dantesque picture made up of a collage of personal items such as shoes, boots, books, maps, golf clubs, flips flops, typewriters, hangers, transistors, cameras, family photographs, slides, tobacco packages, letters, documents and money. Everything was scattered everywhere mingling with the bodies and the charred airplane debris.

Víctor could do little else there except to ask God to have mercy on the souls of these people. He was exhausted after having spent all night without sleeping, so he returned home for a well deserved rest. It was not easy to sleep, on the one hand he was happy they had been able to save a fellow man, but on the other hand he couldn´t remove from his head that on that moonless night in the Alcarria, twenty-four American people had lost their lives.

CAUSES OF THE ACCIDENT

On September 5, 1973 an Aircraft Accident Board at Scott Air Force Base was established to carry out the Safety Investigation of the C-141A 38077 aircraft crash that occurred in Hueva, Guadalajara province, near the Torrejon Air Base, Spain on August 28, 1973.

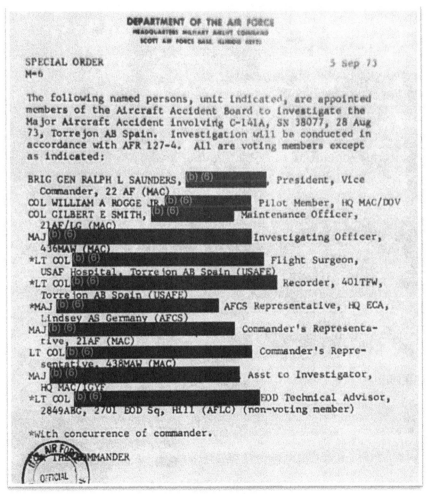

Safety Investigation Board

The investigation was carried out following the protocols implemented in the AFI 91-204 (AFR 127-4, Investigating and Reporting US Air Force Mishaps). The purpose would be, once all the available information was collected, to submit a list with findings, to determine the causes of the accident and to suggest recommendations which could prevent failures for future missions.

In the aftermath of such tragedies, investigators search for causes, hoping to use them to prevent recurrences. The investigation turned up several cause factors in this accident, some of which overlap.

Probably the most critical factor in the sequence of events leading up to the crash of the C-141, that appears in the official accident report, but not in the conclusions of that report, were the communication failures between C-141 M38077 which was broadcasting on VHF and Madrid Control. Madrid Control and the F-4 aircrafts operating out of Torrejon Air Base were transmitting on UHF at the same time they were in communicating with C-141 M38077 on VHF. The UHF communications between the F-4s and Madrid Control overrode or cut off parts of the VHF transmissions between the C-141 and Madrid Control Tower and GCA (Ground Control Approach).

C141 M38077 misheard their descent clearance to 5000 feet as 3000 feet. When 38077 transmitted back their clearance as 3000 feet, they were either not heard or not corrected by Control. In any case, C-141 M38077 continued its fateful descent without further communication from Control.

```
4.  Frequency, landline or position being recorded:

a.  Madrid - 225.4 UHF - M38077

b.  GCA - 125.3 VHF - M38077
         - 266.7 UHF - Duddy 71
         - 385.4 UHF - Balen 61
```

Frequencies of the control tower and aircrafts

This was emphasized by the person responsible for the transcriptions of the communications of the aircraft with the GCA

(Ground Control Approach) in the report of the official investigation:

At 2242 when GCA (Ground Control Approach) was establishing radar contact with Duddy 71 (one of the F-4 fighters), MAC 38077 called GCA on 125.3 VHF simultaneously as GCA was issuing instructions to Duddy 71 on 266.7 UHF. The two transmissions are not two separate distinct broadcasts, but two transmissions heard superimposed on one another.

Seven months after the accident, in March 1974, The Mac Flyer magazine published an article titled "The final error". This article highlights only 4 causes: crew rest, fatigue, discipline and lack of awareness, by chance or intentionally only highlighting causes of the accident which could be viewed as errors by the crew. After my research on all accidents that happened with C-141s throughout its history one can conclude that these four causes by themselves did not cause the aircraft accident. In fact, these errors were not uncommon on many flights and not all of them crashed. The seemingly easiest flights are usually the most dangerous especially when the crew is tired. I'm sure all C-141 pilots who read this will remember night flights, where the crew drank large amounts of strong coffee in order to stay awake.

Picture in the header of the article: "The final error",
from March 1974 Mac Flyer magazine

In 1997 Lt. Col. Paul Hansen developed a flight safety report for the 728th Airlift Squadron from McChord Air Force Base in Washington. The report represents a historical synopsis of all accidents of the Lockheed C-141 Starlifter throughout its history. Its purpose was to familiarize the crews of the C-141 with the history of these aircraft mishaps. The goal was to reduce future mishaps by understanding the accidents that had happened in the past.

Lt. Col. Paul Hansen

Below is the synopsis reproduced in full made by Lt. Col. Paul Hansen about the C-141 that crashed in Hueva in 1973, as it is one of the best I've found:

"During descent for a night GCA approach, the crew misunderstood a descent clearance. Due to communications difficulties, they were unable to confirm the clearance, so accepted what they thought they heard. The aircraft impacted level terrain in a slight descent and was destroyed. Seven crew and 17 passengers were killed. A navigator was thrown clear and survived.

The aircrew departed McGuire AFB for Athens Greece, in mid-afternoon on a planned 23 hour crew duty day, with two enroute stops prior to Athens. The crew arrived in Athens, in the afternoon, and spent the rest of the day sightseeing. They retired to their non air-conditioned hotel for a few hours before doing more sightseeing in the morning. When they departed Athens, that afternoon, on another augmented day back to home station, most were already tired.

28 August was the night of the new moon. The moon had set that evening at 1946 hours Madrid Time. Approaching Torrejon, some hours later, the crew started an enroute descent, for an ILS approach to runway 23 at Torrejon. Weather was reported as 20,000 feet overcast, with 10 NM visibility. During the descent, the pilot noticed that the crew had missed the "Descent Checklist", but became distracted by a radio call and forgot to request it later. The omission went undetected by the rest of the crew.

While level at FL60, the crew was given a clearance to a lower altitude, but because of heavy radio traffic, the clearance was garbled. Although the crew was unsure of whether the controller had cleared them to 5000' or 3000', they agreed between them that it must have been 3000'. They read back "three thousand feet", but the controller missed the error and switched them to the final controller. They again reported "passing 5000 for 3000", but this controller also failed to hear the error. Nearing 3000 feet, the navigator noticed a hill ahead and above their altitude, but the pilot reassured him that "everything looks clear ahead".

The cleanly configured aircraft impacted the level terrain at 250 Knots, near the edge of a plateau at 3050', in a slight descent. The lights of the base were visible in the valley below. The crash killed 7 crew members and 17 passengers. A navigator, in the outboard ACM seat, was thrown clear and survived the accident. At the time of the accident, the crew had spent only eight of the last 60 hours in bed.

Investigators determined that several switches had been left in an incorrect position, indicating the fatigue of the crew.

Because they had omitted the Descent Checklist, the crew had failed to set their altimeters from 29.92" to the local altimeter setting of 30.17" or turn on the radar altimeter. They had not monitored their descent, or noted that a clearance of 3000' was below the glideslope intercept altitude of the ILS approach. Ironically, if the crew had leveled off at 3000' on altitude with their altimeters still set to 29.92", and not allowed the aircraft to descend further, they would still have cleared the terrain by 179 feet."

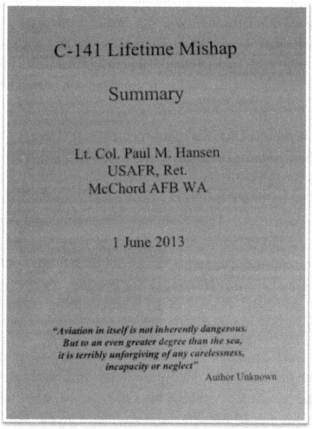

Version 7.0 of the report of all C-141 mishaps,
from Lieutenant Colonel Paul Hansen

The analysis of the C-141 hull-loss mishaps conducted by Lt. Col. Paul Hansen revealed that the most common cause of C-141 mishaps were human errors, with the Controlled Flight into Terrain (CFIT) as one of the most common accidents. Fatigue was a constant hazard of the strategic airlift missions with long duty days and multiple time zones. Air traffic control communication errors or misunderstandings were also main or contributing causes in many accidents. Radio communications were frequently garbled, unclear, overridden by other aircraft, or unintelligible. In the Hueva (aka Torrejon) accident, all these factors came together to form a chain of events that led to the tragic outcome.

IN MEMORIAM THE CREW

The crew of C-141 63-8077 belonged to the 438th MAW (Military Airlift Wing) specifically they were assigned to the 18th MAS (Military Airlift Squadron) at McGuire Air Force Base in New Jersey. At the time of the Hueva accident the 438th MAW had three squadrons assigned to it: the 6th MAS, the 18th MAS, and the 30th MAS.

A normal crew in a C-141 Starlifter consisted of five members: two pilots, one navigator, one flight engineer and one load master. In this flight the crew had been augmented so they could travel further and consisted of eight members: three pilots, two navigators, two flight engineers and one load master.

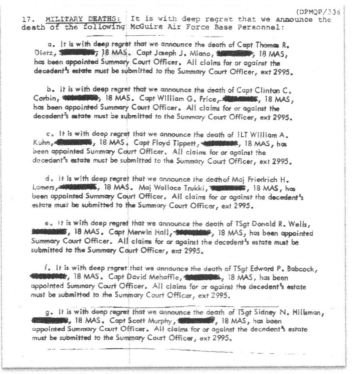

(DPMQP/336)

17. MILITARY DEATHS: It is with deep regret that we announce the death of the following McGuire Air Force Base Personnel:

a. It is with deep regret that we announce the death of Capt Thomas R. Dietz, █████████, 18 MAS. Capt Joseph J. Miano, █████████, 18 MAS, has been appointed Summary Court Officer. All claims for or against the decedent's estate must be submitted to the Summary Court Officer, ext 2995.

b. It is with deep regret that we announce the death of Capt Clinton C. Corbin, █████████, 18 MAS. Capt William G. Price, █████████, 18 MAS, has been appointed Summary Court Officer. All claims for or against the decedent's estate must be submitted to the Summary Court Officer, ext 2995.

c. It is with deep regret that we announce the death of 1LT William A. Kuhn, █████████, 18 MAS. Capt Floyd Tippett, █████████, 18 MAS, has been appointed Summary Court Officer. All claims for or against the decedent's estate must be submitted to the Summary Court Officer, ext 2995.

d. It is with deep regret that we announce the death of Maj Friedrich H. Lamers, █████████, 18 MAS. Maj Wallace Trukki, █████████, 18 MAS, has been appointed Summary Court Officer. All claims for or against the decedent's estate must be submitted to the Summary Court Officer, ext 2995.

e. It is with deep regret that we announce the death of TSgt Donald R. Wells, █████████, 18 MAS. Capt Merwin Hall, █████████, 18 MAS, has been appointed Summary Court Officer. All claims for or against the decedent's estate must be submitted to the Summary Court Officer, ext 2995.

f. It is with deep regret that we announce the death of TSgt Edward P. Babcock, █████████, 18 MAS. Capt David Mehaffie, █████████, 18 MAS, has been appointed Summary Court Officer. All claims for or against the decedent's estate must be submitted to the Summary Court Officer, ext 2995.

g. It is with deep regret that we announce the death of TSgt Sidney N. Hillman, █████████, 18 MAS. Capt Scott Murphy, █████████, 18 MAS, has been appointed Summary Court Officer. All claims for or against the decedent's estate must be submitted to the Summary Court Officer, ext 2995.

Official briefing note from McGuire Air Force Base in the United States with the list of the deceased crew

Clinton Clifford Corbin – Captain, Pilot (Deceased)

Thomas R. Dietz – Captain, Pilot (Deceased)

William A. Kuhn – First Lieutenant, Copilot (Deceased)

Edward Peter Babcock – Technical Sergeant, Flight Engineer (Deceased)

Donald R. Wells – Technical Sergeant, Flight Engineer (Deceased)

Friedrich Hugo Lamers – Major, Navigator (Deceased)

William Haskel Ray – First Lieutenant, Navigator (Survivor)

Sidney Nathaniel Hillsman – Technical Sergeant, Load Master (Deceased)

CLINTON CLIFFORD CORBIN was born on August 26, 1946 in Seattle, Washington. After graduating from Southwest Texas State in 1969 and facing a military obligation, Corbin joined the Air Force. He was an USAF Captain and a pilot. His father was Wayne D. Corbin Major USAF retired and his mother was Roberta H. Corbin (1919-2008). He had three brothers William O. Corbin, Patrick F. Corbin and Thomas A. Corbin. His funeral was held on September 6, 1973 at Fort Sam Houston National Cemetery in San Antonio, Bexar County, Texas, USA.

He died in Hueva, Guadalajara province, Spain on August 28, 1973 at the age of 27 years.

CAPT. CORBIN

THOMAS R. DIETZ was born on August 18, 1947 in Milwaukee, Wisconsin. He lived with his wife at McGuire AFB. His father was Henry Dietz (1918-2003) and his mother Violet Brunner Dietz. He had a sister Patricia S. (Chuck) Impastato and one brother Timothy John Dietz. Thomas was remembered by his father as a born leader. He worked hard at everything. He studied at St. Olaf's College in Northfield, Minnesota and paid for all his expenses through college, graduating in 1969, then entering the Air Force. He was an USAF Captain and a pilot. He is buried in Burlington New Jersey, USA.

He died in Hueva, Guadalajara province, Spain on August 28, 1973 at the age of 26 years.

CAPT. DIETZ

WILLIAM A. KUHN was born on November 28, 1949 in Northport, Long Island in New York. His mother was Ellen G. Kuhn. William was a good athlete and was on the wrestling team at Notre Dame College. He was an USAF First Lieutenant and a co-pilot.

He died in Hueva, Guadalajara province, Spain on August 28, 1973 at the age of 23 years.

LT. KUHN

EDWARD PETER BABCOCK was born on July 30, 1935 in Stockbridge, Windsor County, Vermont USA. His father was George Elvertine Babcock (1900-1967) and his mother Edith Mary Coutre Marsh (1899-1990). He was an USAF Flight Engineer Technical Sergeant. He is buried in Maplewood Cemetery in Stockbridge, Windsor County, Vermont, USA.

He died in Hueva, Guadalajara province, Spain on August 28, 1973 at the age of 38 years.

SGT. BABCOCK

DONALD R. WELLS was born on October 8, 1942. He was an USAF Flight Engineer Technical Sergeant. He is buried in the Laurel Cemetery in Laurel, Clermont County, Ohio, USA.

He died in Hueva, Guadalajara province, Spain on August 28, 1973 at the age of 30 years.

SGT. WELLS

FRIEDRICH HUGO LAMERS was born on August 8, 1933 in Windthorst (Bosnia). He was married to Ruth Lamers and had two children Carla 12 years and Steven 9 years. He was an USAF Major and a Navigator. He is buried in Fort Snelling National Cemetery in Minneapolis, Hennepin County, Minnesota, USA.

He died in Hueva, Guadalajara province, Spain on August 28, 1973 at the age of 40 years.

Biography written by his son Steven Lamers:

"Hello, My name is Steven Fritz Lamers. I am the son of Major Friedrich (Fritz, Fred, Itzy) Hugo Lamers, born on August 8th, 1933 and died August 28th, 1973. My father was one of two navigators and the highest ranking officer on the C-141 that crashed in a field on approach to Torrejon, AFB. As is detailed in this book. I was about two weeks shy of my ninth birthday when we all lost my father.

Friedrich Hugo Lamers was born in Windthorst, Bosnia on August 8th, 1933, (sharing a birthday with his father) and baptized at St. Joseph Catholic Church in Nova Topola, Jugoslavia. As the tenth of twelve children born to Friedrich Gottfried and Anna Hendrina Lamers, Fred grew up in a busy family. The Lamers' family were successful German colonists for six decades and owned three graining mills. Fred at an early age, would often count the money for the business. Friedrich G., Fred's father was a popular man and well respected among the colonists as he had a reputation as an honest man and one who got things done. He was head of the civil defense for the Colony. In 1944, Tito's forces moved in on the town and sent the family to flee in the middle of the night. An account of this is highlighted in F.G Lamers book: "65 Jahre Kolonie In Bosnia, Yugoslavia".

The family arrived in Vienna, Austria and brought to a refugee camp in the Alps in 1944. A couple years later Friedrich G. was able to bring his family to the United States of America. Settling in in the city of St. Paul, Minnesota, the whole family pitched in. Friedrich G. worked on sponsoring other Colonist families from Bosnia, to immigrate to Minnesota. Fred as a teenager was one of the first to have a job bringing in money to help the family that lost everything when they fled Yugoslavia. Fred for a time set up the pins at a local Bowling Alley (pre-machine setters).

In 1956, started by brothers Joe and Fred and friends from immigrant families including Fred Langenfeld and Leo Van Dyck, a soccer club was born and it would be one of the first in the state and would help bring the popular European sport to the Mid-West of the United States. The first meeting took place in April 1956 where it was determined to name the club, "The Saint Paul Soccer Club", name the team the "Blackhawks" and picked team colors of Black and White with alternating Red. Fred ("Fritz") acted as executive secretary. The team also included two from Czechoslovakia and one from Norway and one from Hungary. In the early days the team would have to travel as far as Chicago to find a match.

Original Team — May '52: Back Row - L to R: Fred & Joe Lamers, Adolph & Rudi Hartignaccu, Steve Jenscock, Front Row - Kurt Fechter, Captain, Leo van Dyck, Franz Fechter, Joe Goerges, Alois Langenfeld. Front - Center: Fred Langenfeld

ST. PAUL SOCCER CLUB
The First Fifty Years

Fred was always busy. In Stillwater, Minnesota he took a job at the classy and historic Lowell Inn, where he was able to get his two cousins, Hermann and Gottfried jobs there as well. Fred decided to enter the R.O.T.C. (Reserve Officers Training Corps) instead of enlisting in mandatory military service, thus entering St. Thomas College in St. Paul for a four year education studying language. Upon graduation, Fred would become a commissioned officer in the United States Air Force, a Lieutenant, and owe the military a certain number of years. Little did he know that the Vietnam Crisis and War was soon to begin.

Fred met his soon to be future wife, Ruth Hedwig Thron, born April, 3rd, 1931 to William and Hedwig Thron in Minnesota. They met at a dance at the University Club in St. Paul or right near at the "Germanic Institute or Volksfest House". Fred was stationed in Texas near San Antonio at Harlingen, Air Force Base. Friedrich H. married Ruth H. Thron on October 8th, 1958. Honeymooning across the border in Matamoros, Mexico, even Fred's father came along (discovering the foods spiciness had virtually no effect on him!).

A daughter, Carla Anna Lamers was born unto the happy newlyweds on May, 1st, 1959 in San Antonio, Texas. Soon, after the heightened tensions of the Cuban Missile crisis, where Fred worked in the Strategic Air Command program, he was again transferred to Kansas for a brief stint before ending up in Columbus, Ohio at Lockbourne, AFB. On September 13th, 1964, a son was born, Steven Fritz Lamers. Fred snuck to change the middle name on his birth certificate from Fred to his nickname 'Fritz' while Ruth was in recovery. After just a couple years, leaving a nice home, Fred was again transferred. This time to Norton, A.F.B. in San Bernardino, California. Packing up the car and family and sending the moving truck, Fred drove the family a couple thousand miles to Southern California.

This was a place to stay for awhile, six years. This was the height of the Vietnam war and Fred was gone a lot. When home in San Bernardino, Fred enjoyed the weather and local Mountains. He would often take the family up for drives in the mountains. He loved the neighborhood friends and the friends from base, often enlisted guys.

Vietnam however overshadowed things. Norton AFB was a MAC Military Airlift Command base. Fred went through multiple tours, lasting six months, one... stationed out of Thailand, for a full year. Fred bought himself a bicycle and would leave the base and travel to the village, where he learned the language, made many friends and took many photos. This was not something that was common since most of the servicemen just remained on the base. He had a fond interest for many things including but not limited to, photography, art projects, sketching, the study of foreign language in which he spoke quite a multiple of them fluently and parts of many others.

Major Friedrich H. Lamers was often in the "thick" of things in Vietnam but made it home safely and did not have to return in a combat capacity in 1973.

Then... Fred was asked again to transfer again, and although he wanted to remain in California and be transferred to Northern California, he was told he was needed in New Jersey at McGuire AFB. So he and Ruth sold the house again, sent out the two moving trucks and drove the family across from the west coast to the east coast, a 3000 mile trek made even longer since they stopped in Minnesota for a visit with family and friends.

Upon arrival at Fort Dix McGuire AFB, they settled into the Officers quarters. Fred and Steven in one room and Ruth and Carla in the adjoining room. The search for a house went fairly quick, approximately 20 minutes away in Willingboro, a two story house in a nice neighborhood. Soon the children had to be enrolled in school. Fred took the family on a rare day off on an day trip to Philadelphia, Pennsylvania to see Independence Hall, the place where the Declaration Of Independence was signed and the Liberty Bell. Ruth and Carla enjoyed the rest of the day shopping while Fred took Stevie to a Soccer match at the Stadium. This, from a letter written by Fred from overseas to close friends back in California, "P.S. Stevie and I went to see a soccer game in Phil. May have to see more of those once I get settled." July 4th, 1973.

One night after only a few months in New Jersey while Ruth and the two kids were home, as Fred was away on a routine flight, Stevie was asleep, but Ruth and Carla heard the knock on the front door shortly before 10:00 PM. Seeing a silhouette of two men and the uniform, Ruth instantly knew this was not good news. The men told her the news about Fred and the crash. They said they were wanting to get there before the local nightly news. In the morning, Ruth told Stevie. Soon relatives arrived to help the family and Ruth. Fred's sister Hildegard and Ruth's younger brother Raymond Thron and his wife Diana.

The memorial service and funeral was on September 11th, 1973 at Fort Snelling National Cemetery in Minneapolis, Minnesota. In attendance were his wife Ruth, Children, Carla and Steven, his father Friedrich G. Lamers and a large amount of family, relatives and friends. A 21 gun salute and the folding of the flag which had been draped over the coffin, presented to his widow were very memorable. There was a reception held at the Germanic Center or Volksfest House in St. Paul. Ruth decided to move the family back to San Bernardino, California, where they had lived the longest as a family. Ruth and Steven still live in San Bernardino and Carla lives in Novato, California with her family.

21 gun salute

My words as a last note: I recall at the funeral standing in front of my Uncle Ray and watching so many of my beloved family crying. I was not able to cry that day. This bothered me for a time. I cried before and after just not that day or during the service. My father became an even bigger hero to me that day and has been an inspiration in my life! It was an honor to be able to say a few words about him. Far too few to even encapsulate such a great man and his many good deeds and gifts he left behind and the mark on so many lives he touched. Especially his son. I love you Dad!"

Steven Fritz Lamers October 2016

Major Friedrich Hugo Lamers

SIDNEY NATHANIEL HILLSMAN was born on May 19, 1932 in Geneva, Seminole County, Florida, USA. He was an USAF Technical Sergeant and a Load Master. He was married to Lois M. Hillsman and had three children Cynthia 12 years, Rodney 10 years and Lisa 6 years. The citation that went with his Distinguished Flying Cross and Cluster Air Medal said he showed "personal bravery" flying "extremely hazardous missions through adverse weather with the threat of enemy ground fire and attack". But through all his letters from Vietnam, he never mentioned danger. An Air Force friend remembered him as "quiet and efficient" a "family man" who liked children and coached the base Little League Team. He is buried in the Stewart Memorial Grounds Cemetery in Geneva, Seminole County, Florida, USA.

He died in Hueva, Guadalajara province, Spain on August 28, 1973 at the age of 41 years.

Technical Sergeant Sidney Nathaniel Hillsman

Stewart Memorial Grounds Cemetery

Arlington National Cemetery

IN MEMORIAM THE PASSENGERS

The passenger list had always been a mystery in Spain, since the names of the seventeen passenger casualties were never published in any Spanish journalistic medium. In the United States the names were published in the Trenton Times (the local newspaper for the McGuire AFB area) but I wouldn't discover this information until July 8, 2016.

One of the purposes of writing this book was to find the names of the passengers. After a long investigation looking for the list in the United States with the help of Bill Ray, a clue from José Manuel "Chaska" led us in the right direction and with the help of Víctor Martínez Viana the complete list of passengers was obtained in Spain. Later I received the list with the names again from the report of the official investigation obtained by William in the United States.

Below are listed the names of all passengers with all the information I could find about them. During my research I managed to locate some of the relatives and friends of the deceased passengers, who have collaborated in writing their biographies. Unfortunately I could not locate next of kin of all the deceased passengers so some of the biographies are less extensive.

EDWARD ANTHONY FANELLI was born in California on August 4, 1948. His father was Anthony Edward (Ted) Fanelli (1925-2011) and his mother Beverly Jane Fanelli (1929-2003). He had a sister Tami Anne Fanelli who was 11 when he died. Corporal (E-4) US Marines Retired. He died in Hueva, Guadalajara province, Spain on August 28, 1973 at the age of 25 years. The passport and most of his personal effects were burned in the accident, only one ring and several papers were found and left in custody at the American Consulate. He is buried at Holy Cross Catholic Cemetery in Colma, San Mateo County, California, USA.

Letter written by Edward "Ted" Fanelli to his family:

"Hi everyone,

I know I'm a little delinquent in writing. But to be honest letters haven't been one of my better assets. I don't think I'll be home in August. I'm so involved in my work down here that they strongly suggested I wait awhile.

I miss Tiger. How are you doing Tami? I haven't received a letter from you in a long time. Are you taking good care of your Daddy? What do you want for your birthday? Let me know.

Well as for my well-being, I'm momentarily content. I'm going around Jacqueline Jones quite steadily. My motorcycle is sick (no compression). Doug flew down a few weeks ago. Now he is more inspired than ever not to be drafted. Marty is 1-A. They both are mad at Tim for getting 4-F so easily.

You know you were right. Once you leave home there is no more home. I'm glad I was held off till I was little mature. Now I am on my own and I deeply feel responsible for my own well-being. It sounds ridiculous maybe but What if I didn't? I have done a lot of things in the past that hurt people but it seems they really affect me more in the long run. Guess what I'm trying to say is thank you Mom and Dad for what you have done for me and now that I'm facing the world myself I feel through your past discipline, patience, and understanding I can establish a place for myself. I don't intend any more to be a burden on you, but someone you can rely if you ever need me.

Well Mom, Dad, Tami my eyes are becoming quite indignant about being open so early in the morning. Love, Ted."

Edward Anthony Fanelli

AUSTIN FREDERICK BALKMAN was born on April 8, 1914 near Paris, in Arkansas. Son of John Robert Balkman (1871-1954) and Ocie M. Freeman Balkman (1877-1967). He grew up on a farm with his two brothers, Alton and John Paul. All three brothers went from the farm to the Army, had 30 years of service and attained the rank of Colonel in the Army. Austin was a highly decorated soldier in World War 2 and served in both, the Europe and Africa campaigns. Prior to his death, he had retired from the US Army with Lieutenant Colonel rank and was living in Oklahoma City, OK. He never married and had no children. He had 7 nieces and one nephew, Austin was their favorite uncle and often brought them gifts from his many travels around the world.

Twin brother of Alton F. Balkman, who at that time was a Colonel in the US Army, on active duty working with the Arkansas National Guard and in 1973 lived in N Little Rock, Arkansas (1914-2001). His younger brother, John Paul Balkman, also a Colonel, who in 1973 lived in Springfield, Arkansas (1916-1995). His sister, Mildred Balkman N. Wright, who died the same year as her brother, in Paris, Logan County, Arkansas (1904-1973). His passport and most of his personal effects were burned in the accident, only several papers and mail were found and left in custody at the American Consulate.

He died in Hueva, Guadalajara province, Spain on August 28, 1973 at the age of 59 years.

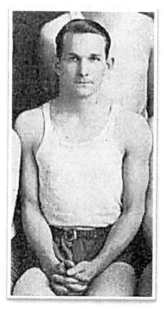

Austin Balkman receiving a Certificate of Appreciation

Austin with his sister, Mildred, and brothers, Alton and John Paul

TERESA ANN WILCOX was born on May 5, 1953 in Westerly, Rhode Island. Her father was Major Robert Edwin Wilcox (August 29, 1930 - June 3, 1988) assigned to JUSMAG (Joint United States Military Aid Group) in Athens, Greece and her mother was Mattie. Her passport and most of her personal effects were burned in the accident. She is buried in the Carolina Baptist Church Cemetery in Covington County, Alabama, USA.

She died in Hueva, Guadalajara province, Spain on August 28, 1973 at the age of 20 years.

DONALD LEE RHODES was born May 10, 1952 in Bonne Terre, Missouri. He was the first of 4 children born to Illa Faye and Herbert Lee Rhodes. He lived his entire life in Farmington, Missouri, until he joined the United States Navy two months after graduating from Central High School, in Flat River, Missouri. He played football and basketball in senior high school, where his number 72 jersey was retired after he died. Donald "Dusty" attained the rank HT2 Petty Officer (Hull Maintenance Technician Second Class) in the Navy and was serving on USS Shenandoah.

His mother, Illa, remembers when Donnie first went to his duty station at San Diego, California. It was the first time he had ever seen the ocean. The seagulls were fascinating to a young boy from Missouri. He was so excited when he came home on leave to see family and friends. He told everyone about his walks on the beaches watching the gulls. It was at that time, he explained that when he was dead, he would come back as a seagull. Flying free to observe everything forever, just like in the book "Jonathan Livingston Seagull".

Donnie, as family members and friends referred to him, was loved by everyone. He never met a stranger and if he did, they parted as friends. Summers were spent at Clearwater Lake, where he loved water skiing and fishing. Donnie married Cynthia Marie Vargo in June 1973 in Elizabeth City, NC, just one month before he left on deployment. They had no children.

Donnie was aboard that fateful flight to return to Missouri to attend the funeral of his maternal grandmother, Mrs. Rose Leatherman of Esther, who passed away one day after attending the wedding of his sister. He was survived by his Mother, Illa Faye Rhodes Lake of Ste. Genevieve, Missouri; his only sister Bonita Faye DeLeal of Sierra Vista, Arizona; and 2 brothers, James Curtis Rhodes of Potosi, Missouri; and David Wayne Rhodes of the home in Farmington, Missouri. His grave is in the Worksmen Park Hills Cemetery in St. Francois County in Missouri.

Biography written with the help of Illa, Bonita, David and Chuck.

He died in Hueva, Guadalajara province, Spain on August 28, 1973 at the age of 21 years.

Donald Lee Rhodes

CHARLES (CHUCK) EDWARD HYATT was born on February 17, 1934 in Waterloo, Seneca County, New York. Charles Hyatt was the son of Skaneateles County Legislator, Arthur W. Hyatt (1904-1999) and Dorothy T. Hyatt (1906-1994).

Hyatt, a 1951 graduate of Skaneateles Central School also attended The Manlius School. He was a graduate of Springfield College and joined the Navy following graduation.

Charles was a carrier-based Naval pilot that served two tours in Vietnam (1966-1968) flying off the USS Intrepid. Hyatt was the Commander of VS-28, an Air Anti-Submarine Warfare squadron stationed aboard the USS Independence in the Mediterranean at the time of his death. He was on his way to join his family in Orange Park, Florida (outside Jacksonville), when the plane crashed in Hueva.

Hyatt was survived by his parents; a sister, Eleanor, and a brother, John (Jack) David Hyatt, all of Skaneateles; his wife, Virginia (1936-1999); a son, Timothy William; and three daughters Tamela Anne, Teri Lynn (1963-2005) and Tracy Elizabeth. His grave is at Arlington National Cemetery, Washington, DC.

Biography written with the help of his brother, Jack and his daugter, Tamela.

He died in Hueva, Guadalajara province, Spain on August 28, 1973 at the age of 39 years.

CMDR. CHARLES HYATT

WILLIAM MOORE O'CONNOR was born on May 15, 1939 in Miami, Florida. He graduated from Miami High School and enlisted in the Navy July 6, 1960. His parents were Nancy Ruth and William Moore O'Connor Sr. William had one brother John Michael O'Connor.

William was married in February 4, 1961 with Clarice Juliette O'Connor (born June 30, 1942). They had 5 children: William Moore O'Connor III, born January 11, 1962; Virginia Ruth O'Connor, born December 29, 1962; Michael Joseph O'Connor, born

February 10, 1966; Thomas Patrick O'Connor, born August 18, 1967; and John Alan O'Connor, born October 26, 1970. His wife Clarice never remarried. She felt her hands were full raising the children (one being disabled). His grave is in Saint Joseph Cemetery in West Greenwich, Kent County, Rhode Island.

Biography written with the help of his wife, Clarice and his daughter, Virginia.

He died in Hueva, Guadalajara province, Spain on August 28, 1973 at the age of 34 years.

William O'Connor's family

SANDRA RAE CANTON maiden name Dennis, was born on February 21, 1950. She attained the rank Corporal in the US Army. She was married in El Paso, Texas, on September 4, 1970 to Barry Gale Canton. She died with her husband in Hueva Guadalajara province, Spain on August 28, 1973 at the age of 23 years. Her grave is in Fort Bliss National Cemetery in El Paso, El Paso County, Texas.

BARRY GALE CANTON was born on August 14, 1948. He attained the rank of Sergeant in the USAF. His parents were Lois Gertrude Hanson Canton (1917-1968) and John Artillo Canton (1918-2001). He was married on September 4, 1970 to Sandra Rae Dennis. He died with his wife in Hueva, Guadalajara province, Spain on August 28, 1973 at the age of 25 years. He was buried on September 10, 1973. His grave is in Fort Bliss National Cemetery in El Paso, El Paso County, Texas.

GEORGIA LORD maiden name Pasoula, was born on April 23, 1951 in Greece. Her parents were Eleni and Vassilis Pasoula from Agia Varvara, Attica, Greece. She was married on September 3, 1972 in Athens, Greece, to Charles Edward Lord.

Georgia died with her husband in Hueva, Guadalajara province, Spain on August 28, 1973 at the age of 22 years.

CHARLES EDWARD LORD was born on November 27, 1936 in Gary, Lake County, Indiana, USA. His parents were Charlotte (Parks) and Harry Lord. He was married three times, first, in 1960 to Elizabet Meyerink, second, to Barbara Eagle and third, to Georgia Pasoula on September 3, 1972.

Charles died with his wife in Hueva, Guadalajara province, Spain on August 28, 1973 at the age of 36 years.

MONTEAL MASSEY maiden name Monteal Fuquay, was born on August 18, 1928 in Wicksburg, Mississippi. Her parents were Irene V. Fuquay (Coley) and Seldon C. Fuquay. Her name appears in 1952 as Monteal Hill, in July 1964 as Monteal Slocum and in April 1971 as Monteal Massey.

Monteal died with her husband in Hueva, Guadalajara province, Spain on August 28, 1973 at the age of 45 years.

FRANK BULLARD MASSEY was born on July 22, 1937 in Lubbock County, Texas, USA. His father, Theodore (Ted) Edward Massey, died in 1998 and his mother, Johnnie Carnelia Price, died in 1987. A brother, Charles Lloyd Massey, died in 1955. Frank attained the rank of Staff Sergeant. He is buried in the Evergreen Memorial Park Cemetery in Tucson, Prima County, Arizona, USA.

He died with his wife, Monteal Massey, in Hueva, Guadalajara province, Spain, on August 28, 1973 at the age of 36 years.

JANICE LYNN BARRON maiden name Janice Lynn Elrod, was born on January 28, 1952 in Memphis, Shelby, Tennessee, USA. Her parents were Sybil Ardella Tedford (1924-2007) and Phillip B. Elrod (1921-2010). She had two brothers Philip S. Elrod and Arthur B. Elrod.

She died with her husband, Clifford Elbert Barron, in Hueva, Guadalajara province, Spain on August 28, 1973 at the age of 21 years.

Janice Lynn Barron

Clifford and Janice Barron

CLIFFORD ELBERT BARRON was born June 30, 1952. His parents were Elnora and Elbert Barron.

He died with his wife, Janice Lynn Barron, in Hueva, Guadalajara province, Spain on August 28, 1973 at the age of 21 years.

MICHAEL L. MERRICKS was born on October 2, 1953 in New Orleans, Louisiana, USA. His parents were Rosalee J. Merricks and William (aka Willie) Merricks. Michael attended George Washington Carver High and after graduation in 1971, enlisted in United States Navy.

He died in Hueva, Guadalajara province, Spain on August 28, 1973 at the age of 19 years.

This is the only photo of Michael preserved by his family, after Hurricane Katrina in 2010

ROBERT L. HOLLOWAY was born on November 14, 1943. He married Kathleen M. Moniz on August 26, 1967 in Alameda City, California, USA.

He died in Hueva, Guadalajara province, Spain on August 28, 1973 at the age of 29 years.

CHRIS LOUIS KATSETOS was born on August 27, 1943. Attained the rank of Lieutenant US Navy Diver. He was posthumously awarded a PhD in Ocean Engineering from the University of Rhode Island. He died in Hueva, Guadalajara province, Spain on August 28, 1973 at the age of 30 years.

CHRIS KATSETOS

Biography written by his friend James Orzech:

"Lieutenant Chris Louis Katsetos, United States Navy, died as a passenger in the crash of a U.S. Air Force C-141 aircraft in Hueva, Spain, near Torrejon AF Base, in August 1973. The flight had originated in Athens, where Chris had been on leave from the Navy, visiting family members in Greece, prior to returning to the University of Rhode Island to complete his graduate studies in Ocean Engineering. As an active duty Naval Officer, Chris had boarded the ill-fated aircraft in a "Space-A" (stand-by) status, as the first leg of his trip home to Rhode Island.

While a Midshipman at the U.S. Naval Academy in Annapolis, Maryland, Chris distinguished himself as the first person to graduate from USNA both with a Bachelors and a Masters degree. Chris also was an accomplished competitive sailor in Flying Dutchman boats, an Olympic-class very fast small sloop with a crew of two, rigged with a spinnaker. Prior to becoming a member of the Class of 1968, Chris already had completed three years of studies at the University of Rhode Island.

According to his classmate at Classical High School in Providence, William Murphy, who knew him well up to 1964, Chris was a very active and curious person, who liked to be "on the edge", racing boats and cars, having a wide variety of interests, but with little trouble with academics. Chris was a natural leader who always aspired to attend the Naval Academy. Although Chris already had been turned down more than once and was close to graduation from the University of Rhode Island, he opted to leave it all behind when an appointment to Annapolis finally came through on his third try.

In 1964 there was very little diversity at the Naval Academy with just eight African American Plebes. There were no women mids then or for many more years. During that period our nation was wresting with its national identity and with civil rights, as well as fighting the Cold War and the War in Vietnam. Lyndon B. Johnson was the Commander in Chief, having assumed his office through the assassination of President John F. Kennedy. Our Class was at the Naval Academy from 1964 through 1968 – right in the middle of the turbulent Sixties and the Vietnam War. There were events during our tenure as midshipmen, such as the assassination of Dr. Martin Luther King, Jr., when the Academy grounds were shut down and patrolled by armed guards due to civil unrest. Senator Robert F. Kennedy, then a Presidential candidate, was shot by an assassin the evening before our graduation and died on our graduation day – June 5, 1968.

In 1995 I was working at the Naval Historical Center in Washington, D.C. One of our staff Historians, Robert J. Schneller, Jr., was writing a book about racial integration at the U.S. Naval Academy to be titled Blue & Gold and Black. I asked him to interview me about the relationship that I observed between Chris Katsetos and Emerson Carr, one of only eight blacks in our class. Schneller wrote, ironically on page 68:

In one extraordinary case, a white plebe used his body to shield a black classmate from racially motivated mistreatment. During plebe year 1964/65, Chris L. Katsetos a white plebe from Rhode Island, James K. Orzech, a white plebe from a suburb of Cleveland, and Emerson F. Carr, a black plebe from Minneapolis, were assigned to the same squad. Orzech had grown up in a place where white people did not want black people moving into their neighborhoods, and he had interacted only infrequently with black people before, so he was a bit standoffish with Carr. But Orzech was still surprised when a few of his white classmates openly expressed their resentment of a black midshipman by making racist remarks. Even more surprising to Orzech was the attitude of Chris Katsetos. While virtually every other plebe tried his best to remain invisible, Katsetos would deliberately provoke upperclassmen. "Who is this nut case Katsetos?" Often Orzech wondered. After plebe summer, Katsetos, Orzech and Carr joined the 14th Company. Soon, the three of them found themselves coming around together to a room occupied by upperclassmen from the Deep South. "They were definitely gunning for Carr," recalled Orzech. "I don't ever remember them using a racial slur or anything like that, but you knew damn good and well they were running Carr extra hard because he was a black." It seemed to Orzech that, whenever Katsetos felt that the southerners were going too far, he would deliberately provoke them into punishing him instead of Carr. Orzech remained braced up and tried to blend into the background while all of this was going on. "I was kind of like the innocent bystander," he recalled. "But I got to do all these extra things." The come-arounds lasted for several weeks. Ultimately, they failed to prevent Carr from graduating, but he was turned back into the class of 1969. Katsetos graduated with honors, the first midshipman to graduate with a bachelor's and a master's degree, but died as a passenger in the crash of a military aircraft in 1973. Orzech served thirty years in the Navy and Naval Reserve, retiring as a captain.

Recently I spoke with Emerson Carr, who did not recall that specific incident, since there were so many other things going on back then, but he agreed with the gist of my story.

Page 68 from the book "Blue & Gold and Black" from Robert J. Schneller Jr where it refers to Chris Katsetos

Chris and I were roommates for Second Class (junior) year and for part of First Class year, when Chris also served as the 6th Battalion and then the 32nd Company Commander. I was honored that he asked me to write the biographical sketch that accompanied his photo in the 1968 Naval Academy Yearbook -- Lucky Bag. I wrote:

"Chris, 'the most famous Greek since Zorba,' came to USNA from Providence, Rhode Island after three years at the University of Rhode Island. There he was the notorious Social Chairman of the Theta Chi Fraternity and in his spare time earned a degree in Chemical Engineering. As a seasoned ROTC (Reserve Officer Training Corps) (Army that is), Chris soon became the most militant Plebe (freshman) in the Brigade. With his vast educational background, 'Greek' had no trouble with academics and will be the first Mid to graduate with a Master's Degree. To the Class of '70, Chris was affectionately known as the "Plebe summer" BOOW (Battalion Officer of the Watch) with the mimeographed Form No. 2. (the form used to put a midshipman on report for any sort of violation, usually resulting in that person being restricted to quarters for a specified period of time). First Class cruise found Chris enjoying many months at sea with the Greek Navy. Chris sailed all four years at Navy and was a big favorite with the coaches. Chris was the nut behind the wheel during the great blizzard of '66. Chris will have a highly successful military career, which will know no bounds."

U.S. Naval Academy – 32nd Company -- Class of 1968
Midshipmen 2/c Katsetos (bottom row far right)
and Orzech (to his right) 1967 Lucky Bag

During spring break in 1966, Chris traveled home to Rhode Island in a rental car with several classmates. The return trip to Annapolis happened during the Great Blizzard of 1966. According to classmates Joe Sikes and Bill Washer, it was only through Chris' superior driving skills and "adult supervision" that the group was able to get back to the Naval Academy in good shape and on time. The next year, Chris and I drove back to his home in his new Corvette. He had experience racing cars, so I learned a few things then, ready or not. To this day I always break in the straight-aways and accelerate in the curves. The news story on the radio on the date of our return, January 27, 1967, was the accident that killed astronauts Gus Grissom, Ed White and Roger Chaffee during a per-launch test in Florida for the Apollo program. Chris and I spent much time on the drive back speculating what it would be like to die suddenly and unexpectedly. Would our thoughts at that instant have enough momentum to reach a conclusion, despite the loss of life? I wonder now what Chris found out.

The last time I saw Chris alive was in June 1970 at the Naval Submarine Base at Ballast Point in San Diego, California, where he was the Diving Officer on USS Ronquil (SS-396), a decorated diesel boat from World War II. It was one of the last diesel boats in the Fleet. In 1973 Chris phoned me to inform me about his upcoming travels to Greece and about his graduate studies at the University of Rhode Island. The Navy had sponsored him, as a Trident Scholar, to build an underwater habitat for scientific research as his Doctoral thesis. By then both Chris and I had attended the Naval School of Diving & Salvage at the Washington Navy Yard. This is the same training that was depicted in the movie Men of Honor. At the time of the mishap in August 1973, I was stationed in San Diego at the Submarine Development Group ONE, also on Ballast Point. I was the Officer in Charge of the Mark 2 Mod 0 Deep Diving System, formerly a part of the Sealab III (underwater habitat) program, as a Saturation Diving Officer. I then was aspiring to go to graduate school at the Scripps Institution of Oceanography in La Jolla, California, which I later did, receiving my Doctorate in Oceanography in 1988. Chris and I had nearly identical professional goals and aspirations, but by strange fate, I was able to live a long life and to accomplish them, but he, by far the more worthy, was not. That has haunted me all along to this day. Chris' precious Navy Diving Officer's pin was recovered from the wreckage at the crash site.

Although Chris was like my big brother and my closest friend, I did not learn of his death for more than three years after the crash. My assignments in the Navy then were very challenging, so I had little time to wonder why I had not heard from Chris. As a member of the U.S. Naval Academy Alumni Association, I somehow had missed seeing his obituary in the December 1973 issue of Shipmate magazine. On page 88 it read:

"Lt. Chris Louis Katsetos, USN, died in an airplane accident in Hueva, Spain. Services were held in the Annuncion Greek Orthodox Church in Cranston, R.I. with burial in the North Burial Ground. Born in Providence, R.I., Lt. Katsetos graduated from the Naval Academy. This was his third college degree, having a Bachelors degree from the University of Rhode Island and a Masters degree from George Washington University. In Annapolis, he was on the Superintendent's list for four years. He was also fluent in Greek and Russian. Lt. Katsetos was stationed in the Pacific for most of his Navy career. He was a member of the board of the Greek Orthodox Church in Greater Providence and a member of the Sophicles Chapter of AHEPA. He was also a member of the American Chemical Society and the Theta Chi Fraternity at the University of Rhode Island. He was an altar boy and also an Eagle Scout and a Sea Scout. He is survived by his mother, Mrs. (Georgiana) Katsetos, 24 Alhambra Circle, Edgewood, R.I."

In the early 1980's I visited Chris' heartbroken parents in Rhode Island and kept in contact with his mother until her death. Both parents were Greek immigrants and Chris was their only child. The parents took me to a family-owned Greek restaurant. Chris' mother was distraught by the loss of her beloved son. I learned only recently that Chris' closed-casket funeral had been a significant news event in Providence. According to classmate John Mortsakis, "In the Greek Orthodox faith, we end our services for the departed with the phrase in Greek: "Eternal be their Memory.""

The Class of 1968 graduated 836 Navy Ensigns or Marine Corps Second Lieutenants from all fifty states and five foreign countries. Our distinguished classmates have experienced marvelous adventures in war and at peace all around the world from in space to the bottom of the sea. Classmates currently in the public eye include the current Chief of NASA, Charlie Bolden; former-Chairman of the Joint Chiefs of Staff, Admiral Mike Mullen; former U.S. Senator, Jim Webb; and television news commentator Oliver North. According to our website, we produced three 4-star, one 3-star and eighteen 2-star Admirals, plus six Marine Corps Generals and three Astronauts. The living members of our class are now in their seventies."

I received recollections of Chris from several classmates, including:

• Bill Ruch recalled: "Chris, Emerson Carr and I were roommates during Plebe Summer. Most of the summer is still a blur to me, but I do remember the intensity Chris had in everything he did, whether it was shining shoes, or making sure Emerson Carr was up early for football practice. First-class year he gave me a ride to Richmond in his Corvette. (Interstate Highway) I-95 was basically brand new and traffic was very sparse. Somewhere north of Quantico, he wanted to see how fast it would go. I glanced up and the speedometer was showing about 110 (miles per hour or about 177 km per hour). ... (In Richmond) I do remember that he charmed my mother with, as she put it, his excellent manners. He was a very intelligent, focused and dynamic gent."

• Jim von Suskil wrote, "I remember Chris well for the reasons that we all probably did. He was just a nice guy and a whole lot more worldly than the rest of us. The incident that I shall always recall hardly had a military impact, but it occurred in February of our second-class year. I had a blind date with a girl who arrived in a VW Beetle. She parked the car in the Yard and then promptly locked the keys in the car. Chris happened upon the scene shortly after we discovered the problem with some dry cleaning over his shoulder. He immediately coughed up a coat hanger that we fashioned into a hook. We took turns fishing for the lock button. I can't remember which one of us was successful, but we got the car door opened on a very cold winter day... End of drill. My wife, Susan, still remembers Chris kindly for getting our first date off on the right foot."

- Jim "Razz" Rather wrote: "I hardly knew Chris Katsetos back at USNA, but I certainly knew of his reputation... But ironically, I was probably one of the last guys from '68 to see him alive. It was in January or February of 1972. I was in VP-24 in (Naval Air Station) Patuxent River (Maryland) at the time and my crew opted to take a weekend cross-country round trip to San Diego. From (Naval Air Station) North Island (Coronado, California) we had a few Space-A passengers for our return, one of which was Chris. Chris was going on leave from the submarine on which he was stationed and the flight to Pax River got him to the East Coast. Chris and I chatted for a long time during the flight, maybe 4 or 5 hours or so. I was surprised that one of our classmates actually got an assignment to a diesel submarine. There weren't many of those left in the inventory at that time. He was a very impressive officer and I sensed that he would go far in his Navy career. He had success written all over him. I didn't hear of his death for several years. Man was I shocked and saddened by the news. Just goes to show there are no guarantees in life."

May God bless Chris Katsetos and all the others

who perished so long ago on that ill-fated flight,

Captain James Orzech (aka "Otto") USNR (retired)

United States Naval Academy Class of 1968

September 26, 2016

MEMORIAL CEREMONIES

In the 43 years that have passed since the accident which took place in 1973 near Hueva, Guadalajara province, Spain, only three memorial ceremonies have taken place in honor of the victims.

The first memorial ceremony took place one week after the accident at McGuire AFB chapel in New Jersey, USA. The commander of the 438th Military Airlift Wing (MAW), Brig. Gen. George M. Wentsch and more than 500 airmen, nearly every man on the base who could leave his duty, attended the chapel service in memory of the seven crewmen who perished in the crash of their C-141 cargo jet in Spain. Unfortunately the only survivor First Lt. William H. (Bill) Ray was hospitalized in Walson Army Hospital, Fort Dix, New Jersey following surgery and could not attend, but his parents did.

McGuire Mourns 7 Lost In Spain Crash

McGUIRE AFB — More than 500 airmen attended a chapel service here yesterday afternoon in memory of the seven crewmen who perished in the crash of their C-141 cargo jet in Spain last week.

The solemn event was held while the bodies of the seven men were being readied for shipment at Dover AFB in Delaware to their hometowns across the nation. The bodies arrived at Dover from Spain over the weekend.

Led by the commander of the 438th Military Airlift Wing, Brig. Gen. George M. Wentsch, nearly every man on the base who could leave his duty attended the half-hour ceremony.

In the meantime, Lieutenant William Ray, the plane's navigator and the only survivor of the disaster was flown here Sunday and, a base spokesman said, is in satisfactory condition at Walson Army Hospital at Fort Dix.

In addition to the seven McGuire men who died in the accident, 17 passengers on board the aircraft, dependents of military men, also lost their lives. The plane was en route from Athens, Greece, to Torrejon.

McGuire yesterday held memorial services for the crash victims. Here, some of the hundreds who attended leave the base chapel.

"Trenton Times" newspaper September 5, 1973

105

A few days after the accident, Víctor Martínez Viana could not remove from his head the images of what had happened. He kept mulling over the possibility that perhaps they could have saved more people. Víctor thought that they had to honor those poor people who had lost their lives so close to their town. So he convinced the mayor, Federico Aguirre Plaza, to go with him to Guadalajara to ask for financial assistance from the Governor of the Province, D. Carlos Montoliu and Carrasco (Baron of Albi), to put in place a plaque to remember the victims of the accident. Thanks to these people, the memory of the people who lost their lives during this tragic event can still be honored and remembered.

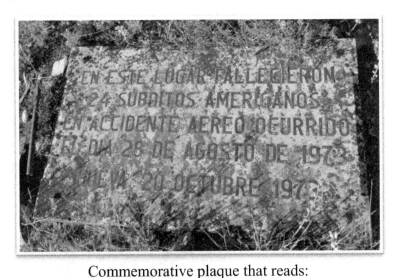

Commemorative plaque that reads:
"In this place died 24 American citizens in a plane crash which ocurred on August 28, 1973. Hueva October 20, 1973"

The second memorial ceremony was held in the town of Hueva on October 20, 1973. On this occasion in attendance at the ceremony were the Guadalajara Civil Governor, Carlos Montoliu and Carrasco (Baron of Albi), the US American Ambassador, D. Horacio Rivero, General Salvador Saelices USAF, Torrejon Air Base Vice Commander of the 16th Air Force and Chief of Torrejon AFB, Lieutenant General Chief of Staff of the Spanish Air Defense, D.

Ramiro Pascual on behalf of the Spanish Air Minister, the Spanish Head of Torrejon Base, D. Rafael Lorenzo Bellido, and Mr. Rafael Borras, representative of General Vives.

The ceremony was also attended by the sole survivor First Lt. William H. (Bill) Ray who traveled from a military hospital in the United States of America expressly to thank all the people of Hueva and especially Antonio Beas and Víctor Martínez for saving him from certain death.

Emotional hug between Antonio and William

William´s gift to Antonio and Víctor, in gratitude and friendship, Bulova watches. Their friendship has continued over the years despite the distance.

Bulova watches Bill gave to Antonio and Víctor

An official scroll of appreciation, addressed to all the inhabitants of the town, was presented to the City of Hueva during the ceremony. In addition, individual letters of appreciation were presented to Antonio Beas and Víctor Martínez for their extraordinary and heroic efforts in saving the life of First Lt. Ray.

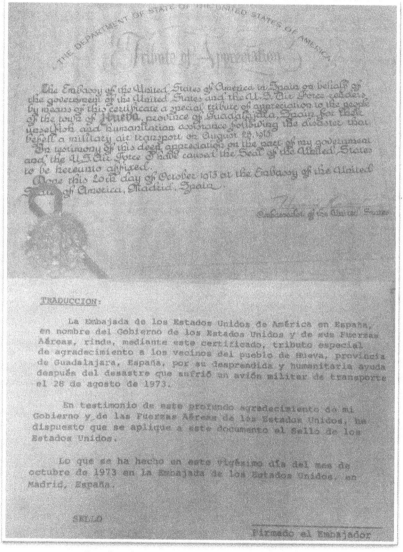

Gratitude Scroll to the town of Hueva

Letters of appreciation from US Embassy in Madrid
and from William A. Evans Colonel, Commander of the
401 Combat Support Group at Torrejon AFB to Antonio and Víctor

110

End of the ceremony with a toast

After the ceremony in Hueva they went to the Governor´s villa in Guadalajara where a meal was served for First Lieutenant William Ray and the American authorities. During the meal one of the Spanish dignitaries removed a pin from his jacket lapel with the shield of Guadalajara, a gold bee and four rubies and gave it to William. This person, whose name William does not remember, made a presentation speech about the plane crashing into olive orchards and said Guadalajara was well known for its honey. He compared the rescue of William by the people of Hueva as a 'rebirth', just as each year the olive trees are brought to life again by the bees producing a new crop of olives. After the meal the Governor presented William with an olla with Guadalajara honey.

Guadalajara shield pin

The third memorial ceremony was performed at McGuire AFB on November 11, 2008, in which active duty military members, reservists, veterans and the civilian community gathered at the site of the new Starlifter C-141 Memorial Park. It is noteworthy that Congressman Jim Saxton, Col. Scott Smith 305th Air Mobility Wing vice commander and Mr. Ted Strempack, President of the Major Thomas McGuire Foundation were in attendance. During this Veterans Day ceremony the memory of all who died in accidents with total loss of the C-141 aircraft operated from McGuire AFB were honored. This ceremony also served as the opening of the "Starlifter Memorial Park" sponsored in part by the Major Tommy B. McGuire Foundation. There are two monoliths, one with all the names of the C-141 deceased crews with a total of 37 servicemen lost in 4 accidents resulting in the complete loss of a C-141 operating from McGuire in 30 years of service. These mishaps are as follows: Tail# 38077 Torrejon, Spain August 28, 1973 with 7 crewmen lost; Tail# 70006 Sondrestorm, Greenland August 28, 1976 with 7 crew lost; Tail# 70008 RAF Mildenhall, England with 14 crewmen lost and Tail# 59405 Near Namibia, Africa September 13, 1997 with 9 crew lost.

McGuire AFB ceremony on November 11, 2008

Additionally, in this park is the first C-141 that was assigned August 8, 1967 to 438th Military Air Wing McGuire Air Force Base, the 66-7947 whose name was "The Garden State Airlifter".

Acceptance Ceremony Charter of the first C-141
"The Garden State Airlifter"

Photos by Bryan McPhee

ANTONIO BEAS

Antonio Beas Pérez de Tudela Enviz was born on October 23, 1945 in El Pardo (Madrid). His parents José and Maria had eight children, Antonio being the third.

Antonio's family at Zaida´s wedding

He entered military service at age 22 at "Campamento San Pedro" (Camp Saint Peter) in Colmenar Viejo as Assistant Instructor and exited at 23, with his military obligation completed.

He went to elementary school and worked as a plumber, but at age 25 he completed the training for and received his electricians' license. His brothers set up a multi-purpose company "Hermanos Beas" (Beas Brothers) in 171 Villamil Street in Madrid where Antonio worked for eight years.

Zayda, Toñin, Chema and Aroa

Around 1975 there was a very large economic crisis in Spain, so Antonio split from his brothers´ company and set up in 1976 a "rural mixed commerce" (a bar with integrated shop on the same premises) called Bar Chispa. Later he began in Hueva a firm of electricians independent from the one in Madrid which continues operating today by his son Antonio.

Chispa Bar

He met his wife Maria Josefa (Pepa) in 1969, marrying in 1970 after eight months of dating. They had five children Zayda born in 1970, Antonio (Toñin) in 1972, Richi in 1974 (deceased), José Maria (Chema) in 1978 and Aroa in 1980. They have 6 grandchildren.

Antonio retired at age 54 and spends time since then at his farm in Hueva, taking care of his hives, working in the garden and occasionally going hunting, as one of his granddaughters says: "doing retired stuff".

Sandra, Raquel, Toñin, Pepa, Bill, Antonio, Saul and Juampi
Zayda, Jacob, Chema, Ricardo, Zayda, Antonio, Aroa,
Cintia and Fede

VÍCTOR MARTÍNEZ VIANA

Víctor Martínez Viana was born on April 20, 1940 into a large family, which was very common in those days. His parent's names were: Francisco and Dionisia. Víctor was the eldest of six brothers. Although born in Peralveche, he grew up with his uncle Angel de Francisco Peinado in Cifuentes; both are towns in the province of Guadalajara (Spain). He has lived in Madrid since 1958, although is linked to Hueva by marriage and maintains a home in Hueva as well.

Brigida and Víctor

When he was young in Cifuentes he joined various organizations, both religious and political. He was the founder of "Tarsicio" and belonged to "Frente de Juventudes" (Youth Front), occupying the post of Head of National Centuria. He has always seen this stage of his life as a wonderful time in which he acquired great principles.

He started working when he was very young. At the age of 12 years he began work as an errand boy in the Property Registry of Cifuentes and later at the Regional Delegation of Tabacalera and correspondents of banks. At 17 he completed an internship at the Regional Court.

In January 1958 he moved to Madrid and he worked in administration, in a transport company, whose owners were from Cifuentes.

In 1960 along with others, Víctor founded the Regional Center House of Guadalajara in Madrid.

In 1964 he was elected as shop steward of the former Spanish Union Organization, occupying various positions in the Provincial and National Association, the National Union of Feeding, the Council of Workers, at the Training College Virgin of the Pigeon and the Workers Provincial Council of Madrid.

He married Brigida on July 25, 1965 in Madrid. A year later his daughter, Eva, was born and six years later his son, Víctor. Currently they have three grandchildren: Rebecca, Adriana and Hector.

Víctor´s family

In 1968 he bought a stand at Barajas market dedicated to dairy products that was run by his wife Brigida, and then by her sister Maria Josefa. It would be here where Antonio Beas would meet Maria Josefa (Pepa) with whom he would be married a few months later.

In 1975 he met Manuel Fraga Iribarne through some friends and was in (GODSA). In 1977 he joined "Democracia Social" (Social Democracy party), from Licio de la Fuentes, which merged with "Alianza Popular" (the Popular Alliance party), finally becoming "Partido Popular" (the Popular Party).

In 1979 he was invited to visit Germany by the Conrad Adenauer Foundation, and also by the United States, as a Spanish trade unionist and founder of the same, with a scholarship by the American Union AFL-CIO.

He collaborated with the University of Murcia in 1981, in celebration of the VII Centenary of Don Juan Manuel, Lord of Cifuentes (Guadalajara). He has participated in several summer courses in the University Rey Juan Carlos of Madrid, also in Trillo (Guadalajara) and Vicalvaro.

In 1995 he was elected by an absolute majority mayor from "Partido Popular" party of the town of Hueva (Guadalajara). During his time at the Town Hall he managed the recognition and approving of the shield of the town. He also founded Dr. Francisco Layna Serrano library. His interest in education led him to push for the release of a book on the history of the Village of Hueva. He was president of the Brotherhood of the Holy Christ of the Faith, patron of the town. He was also founder of the cultural association of "Melchor Lopez Jimenez" favorite son of Hueva, in whose name the town square will be dedicated.

Book: "A History of the Village of Hueva, 2003"

For more than 37 years Víctor wrote articles for the Guadalajara provincial press, especially in "Nueva Alcarria", although he also wrote articles in other newspapers such as "Flores y Abejas" (Flowers and Bees), "Guadalajara 2000", etc. He was also a correspondent for "Radio Juventud Guadalajara" (Radio Youth Guadalajara) in Cifuentes. Currently he continues to make occasional contributions.

In 2009 his journalistic spirit and need for the truth led him to write a research book entitled: "Breve Historia de Fray Diego de Landa" (A Brief History of Friar Diego de Landa), 468 pages, which highlights the full manuscript of 1566. This work is dedicated to the great Universal Cifontino, Friar Diego de Landa Calderón, Bishop of Yucatan, to whom we owe everything we know about the Mayan language. Publication of this book led to an invitation from Dr. Varela to participate as a speaker at the "XX International Congress on discovery and mapping" held at the Center for American Studies at the University of Valladolid, Spain and that would be a very rewarding experience for both, he and his wife, for the treatment received.

He holds several titles and awards, including the Honorary Historian, the "Melero Alcarreño" as founder of the House of Guadalajara. The award medal "La Venera" of the "Cross of the Cardinal Points" by the National Federation of Spanish Naval League.

Víctor offering Gustavo a dedicated copy of his book

Nowadays, being retired as a civil servant since 2005, Víctor has more time to devote to his ongoing research, which has led him to take up a project that he had put on hold for a while, writing a book about "Doña Juana de Silva" from Cifuentes, who eventually will become Princess of Melito and Eboli.

WILLIAM HASKEL RAY

"My name is William Ray. I was the sole survivor of a C 141 aircraft accident that occurred near Torrejon AFB in Spain, in August, 1973...".

Thus began the letter written by William H. (Bill) Ray asking for information from the Pentagon about the official investigation of the accident that occurred in Hueva, a small town in Guadalajara on August 28, 1973.

William Haskel Ray was an average American citizen, but a plane crash during his military service would mark his life forever. He was born June 5, 1948 in Wyandotte, Michigan (near Detroit). He attended the University of Michigan in Ann Arbor, which is about 50 kilometers from Detroit, from August 1966 to May 1970 where he received a Bachelor of Engineering.

First Lieutenant William H. (Bill) Ray
October 20, 1973
Courtesy of Víctor Martínez Viana

124

In 1969 during the height of the Viet Nam war and because the war was so unpopular, the draft was reinstated. The United States reinstated a lottery for the draft. The lottery was considered the fairest way to conscript men into the military. All men over age 18 had to register for the draft for military service. December 1, 1969 marked the date of the first draft lottery held since 1942. This drawing determined the order of induction for men born between January 1, 1944 and December 31, 1950. A large glass container held 366 blue plastic balls containing every possible birth date affecting men between 18 and 26 years old.

Lilia and Bill with their children Andrew and Daniel

Bill's birth date, June 5, drew ball number 28 out of 366. Upon graduation from the University of Michigan he would certainly have been drafted, so he chose to voluntarily enlist in the Air Force where he could earn more money as an officer.

Bill's parents had both served as volunteers in the army during World War II. They met in New Guinea in the Pacific, where his mother worked as a secretary to a physician in a field hospital and his father was an ambulance driver.

Bill was married in February, 1969 to Lilia McBride born in Belfast (Northern Ireland). Her parents emigrated first to Canada and then to the USA.

Lilia and Bill Ray

Five months after finishing the University, in October 5, 1970, He entered the U S Air Force, completing basic training November 20, 1970 and then officer's training approximately February 25, 1971 and finally went to navigator training. He also completed several other shorter training classes such as water survival, winter survival, prisoner of war training, ect. Finally he was assigned to McGuire Air Force Base in New Jersey in the 18th Military Airlift Squadron (MAS) within the 438th Military Airlift Wing (MAW). He flew for the first time as a navigator on a C-141 aircraft in March, 1972.

18th Military Airlift Squadron   438th Military Airlift Wing

Daniel, Allison and Andrew

After the plane crash in August, 1973, Bill spent much time in and out of the hospital, having several surgeries primarily on his left leg and ankle, and was medically retired from the Air Force in August 1974.

He went back to school at the University of Michigan for 2 semesters, receiving a second engineering degree and in May of 1975 Bill started working for the Department of Veterans Affairs as a facilities engineer, where he worked for almost 30 years, retiring in January 2004. He worked at several VA medical centers in different states, but spent the vast majority of his career at the VA medical center in Danville, IL.

Bill and his wife Lilia have a great family with three children Daniel 45, Andrew 43 and Allison 39 and a total of 5 grandchildren.

Lilia and Bill grandchildren

HUEVA (SPAIN)

Hueva, April 12, 2016

Hueva, formerly called Ova, is a Spanish municipality with 140 inhabitants (Census 2015), located in the province of Guadalajara, in the center of the region of La Alcarria. It is distanced 38 km from the capital and 7 km from Pastrana. Hueva shares municipal boundaries with the surrounding towns of Moratilla de los Meleros, Renera, Fuentelencina, Pastrana and Escopete.

Ova was reconquered from the Muslims in the year 1124, during the reign of Alfonso VII of Castille, who donated the town to Garcia Navarro.

Years later, in 1175, the town of Hueva was donated by his successor Alfonso VIII to the Order of Calatrava, which built a castle in the vicinity and from where the lords of the town governed until well into the sixteenth century.

Hueva achieved the status of independent villa around the second half of the fifteenth century, which afforded it such judicial and administrative autonomy as, administration of the municipal budget, choosing two mayors and two council members elected by the residents of the village, and having its own prosecutor, a constable and a notary.

For those who venture to visit the town of Hueva some historical highlights of the village are the Church of Our Lady of the Bramble next to the remains of the medieval wall of the fifteenth century, the Plaza Mayor with the town hall, the Picota monument and a fountain of the twentieth century, the Palace of the counts of Zanini and Saint Roch Hermitage.

The most noted personalities of Hueva include: Melchor Lopez Jimenez, master of the Chapel of Santiago de Compostela for 38 years, who was named favorite son of the town in 1978 and whose name was given to the Plaza Mayor, Alfonso Fernandez, who entered the priesthood in the Monastery of Ucles (Cuenca), and participated in the Council of Trent with the Bishop of Guadix, D. Martin de Ayala that later would become Archbishop of Valencia.

Included below are directions to get to the place where the American aircraft crashed, both for those who want to visit the place for the first time and for all those who were affected in one way or another by the accident and want to return to this place to honor the memory of the deceased.

Church of Our Lady of the Bramble

View of the church from Town Square

An ancient local tradition places the castle of Juan Sanchez in Hueva, on the promontory where the church currently stands. No medieval documents directly endorse this existence except its mention in the books of the church (libros de fabrica) from the sixteenth century and the only remains of the walls that can be seen today are situated at Castle Street "Calle del Castillo".

Remains of the old castle wall

The Church is dedicated to "Our Lady of the Bramble", it consists of a small masonry building with rectangular construction plant. Construction began around the XIII and XIV centuries as evidenced by its semicircular apse of Romanesque design covered by a vaulted dome. In the entrance door we can find two reliefs representing Saint Peter and Saint Paul.

The nave which was renovated in 1798 is covered by a vault of lunettes. Two doors open into the center of the nave. The one to the north of Gothic style of the XIV century and another to the south of the XVI century of Renaissance style. At the bottom of the nave is the tribune for the choir and organ. The bell tower is from the XV century with the baptismal font located at its base from the XVI century.

The 3 tables that are preserved from the artist Juan de Cerecedo

At present, only three tables from the altarpiece of the parish are preserved that survived several fires. They are located on the sides of the nave next to the chapel. The tables were made by the artist Juan de Cerecedo between 1574 and 1582 and represent the scene of the Annunciation to the Virgin Mary, the Presentation in the Temple and the Epiphany or Adoration of the Three Kings.

Next to the parish church stands the Hermitage of the Holy Christ of the Faith, a work of the sixteenth century with numerous renovations, the latest in 2002 by the Brotherhood of Christ. Presiding over the high altar is a carving with the image of the Holy Christ of the Faith who is the patron of Hueva.

Town Square

The Town Square, dedicated in 1978 to Melchor Lopez Ximenez, is the primary open space in the town on which the main buildings are located. In the 85 manuscript of Cardinal Lorenzana from XVIII century it is described as follows:

"The square of this town is in square shape, and in the facade facing at noon are the town halls, the butcher, royal granary and jail, each building with separation, although under the key of the front door, and in the other east facade is the parish church, that was built at the time of the Goths or Moors apparently as a castle."

132

In the Hueva town square are the Town Hall, the pillory monument and a modern fountain constructed in 1926.

Town Hall

In the Town Hall the main functions were the government in the council chamber and public court hearings. One could also find in this building in ancient times: the prison, the municipal archives with the ark of the scriptures, the hospital (which was more a shelter to address the problem of homelessness and begging), a storage of grain, a cellar for wine collection, the butchery and the forge.

Hueva Town Hall, April 12, 2016

Picota or Pillory monument

The first Pillory monument was located just outside the town of Hueva in the direction of Fuentelencina. It was probably a simple wooden pillory and it was not until the sixteenth century that the current pillory (monument) was ordered to be built: A pillory made of stone on four circular steps of rustic stone onto which a cubic pedestal sits whose only adornment is a square etched frame on each of its faces. On that cube stands the base that supports the smooth cylindrical shaft of a column topped with one chapter with three emerging heads of fantastic animals with ghoulish looks and open mouths baring fangs. Another cubic pedestal decorated with triglyphs serves as the base for another grooved cylindrical pedestal.

The Pillory monument structure was restored during the tenure as mayor of Hueva of D. Víctor Martínez Viana. The pedestal was later restored by another corporation.

Pillory in Town Square in Hueva, April 12, 2016

Palace of Zanini´s counts

This is a renaissance-style palace of the XVI century that belonged to the counts of Zanini. The palace has a magnificent facade that combines a marble door with tapila (ancient technique that consisted of constructing walls with wet clay compacted with blows) of the walls. Its interior highlights coffered ceilings and magnificent style tiles.

Palace of the counts of Zanini

Saint Roch Hermitage

The Saint Roch Hermitage (Ermita de San Roque) is located on the road to Fuentelencina outside Hueva. It is a small square building with a porch supported by two pillars guarding the entrance from rain, both covered with tile roofs. The outer walls have no decoration and the Hermitage has a large gabled front door.

Site of the accident

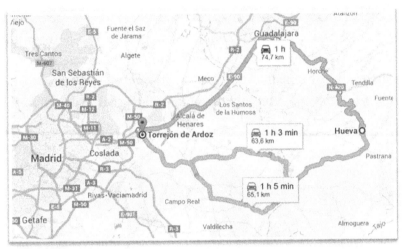

Map with the distance between the towns of Hueva
and Torrejon de Ardoz

Although in some places the accident site is referred to Torrejon as this is the name of the military base where the C-141 aircraft should have landed, in reality the accident site was on a hill near the village of Hueva in the province of Guadalajara, about 60 km away from the airbase of Torrejon.

On the map below you can see Route 1 and Route 2 from Hueva to the nearest access to the crash site. The crash site is in the midst of olive groves and the area is not prepared for visitors, no parking area available, so you have to find a place to park your vehicle that does not block the way to other drivers.

Both routes have as a starting point the town square (Plaza Mayor), continuing along the main street (Calle Mayor) and the Saint Roch road (Paseo de San Roque) taking the detour to the right (about 370 meters) that goes to Fuentelencina passing by the cemetery (about 690 meters).

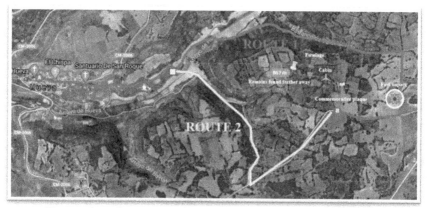

Route 1 and Route 2, from Hueva to the accident site

At 1100 meters from town square (Plaza Mayor) the two routes diverge, the Route 1, follows the road parallel to the Hueva Stream (Arroyo de Hueva) and continues toward Ravine of Valdelacorza (Barranco de Valdelacorza) taking the right road at the fork to 3160 meters. Continue along this road, about 500 meters, turning back to the right and continuing 540 meters, to the nearest place along the road to the commemorative plaque, where one must leave the car continuing on foot.

The Route 2, branches off to the right at 1100 meters, along the Ravine of Saint Mary (Barranco de Santa Maria) continuing until you reach another road (after traveling 1380 meters after leaving the blue route, approximately 2480 meters from town square (Plaza Mayor)) where it turns left and follows about 1000 meters, to reach the nearest place along the road to the accident area, where we will have to walk through the fields about 150 meters to the commemorative plaque.

The best way to get to the crash site is to use a GPS (Global Positioning System) and enter any of the coordinates in the images shown below. Coordinates set by Google Maps. Images courtesy of José Manuel "Chaska", www.hueva.net administrator.

Gustavo Doménech with José Manuel "Chaska"

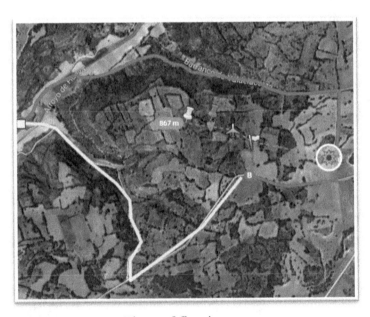

Place of first impact

N 40.461424 W -2.926913

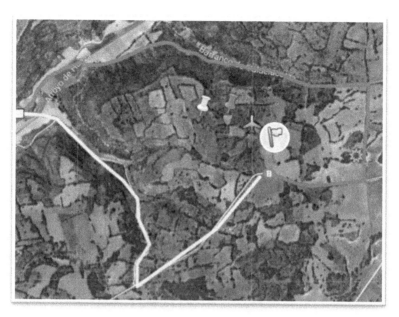

Conmemorative plaque

N 40.462093 W -2.931940 Alt: 1023.1

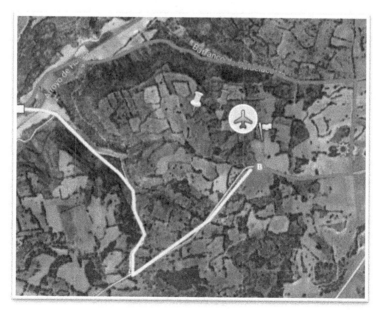

Cabin of the C-141

N 40.462735 W -2.933383 Alt: 1012.5

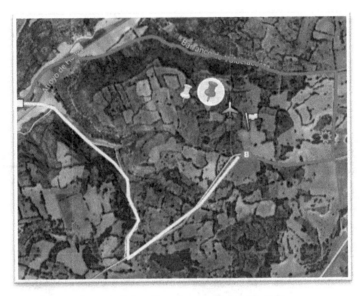

Rest of the fuselage of the C-141

N 40.463128 W -2.934935 Alt: 1002.7

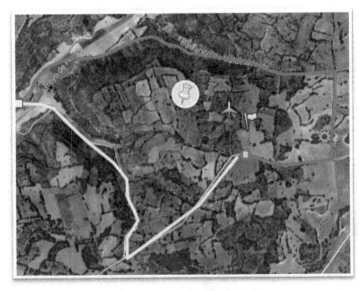

Remains found, farther away from the first impact site,

at 867 meters

N 40.463056 W -2.936667

NEWSPAPERS

In this chapter is provided much of the information I have collected throughout the investigation about the plane crash on August 28, 1973 in Hueva which appeared in the newspapers of Spain and the United States.

Regarding American newspapers, it must be taken into consideration the historical context in which the accident occurred to understand that the news about the accident did not have the same impact on American newspapers that it did in the Spanish press. The Vietnam War, the Watergate case and the imminent Arab-Israeli war permeating the front pages of American newspapers. None of the news that I found in American newspapers, on the crash of C-141 in Hueva, appeared on the front page except in the 'Trenton Times' which was the local paper near McGuire AFB. In the case of the "New York Times" this story appeared in the August 29, 1973 edition on the 13th page, the next day coverage appeared on page 4 with the list of names of the deceased crew members.

Also noteworthy is that, besides the "Trenton Times", the "Detroit Free Press" of August 30, 1973 is the major American newspaper where a photograph with charred wreckage was published. The "New York Times" of August 29, 1973 and the "Chicago Tribune" of August 30, 1973 accompanied the text with drawings of a map of Spain showing the locations of the city of Madrid, Torrejon Air Force Base and the crash site.

The stories in American newspapers are almost exclusively the information received from news agencies, UPI (United Press International) and AP (Associated Press). Thus we find that the information that appeared in the "New York Times" of August 29, 1973 and the "Chicago Tribune" on August 30, 1973 with information from the AP news agency are an exact copy. Likewise the "Desert Sun" of August 29, 1973 and the "Detroit Free Press" August 30, 1973 using information from the UPI news agency are the only ones in which the American pilot of an F-4 is mentioned as a witness to the accident.

Almost all information appearing in American newspapers about the accident, the type of aircraft, crew, passengers, one survivor, etc is correct. There was only one discrepancy in the reporting: Was any child among the dead? In almost all American and Spanish newspapers were reporting that among the victims were women and at least one child. After finding the list with all the names of the deceased, there are no children included in the list. After my investigation, none of the witnesses I interviewed from the rescue teams confirmed seeing the corpse of any child. Mike Sweeney was a surgical assistant sent to the crash site to recognize and identify human remains and he has also flatly denied that any remains of children had been found. One witness, Víctor Martínez Viana said he saw a small doll among the debris of the plane and assumed it might have belonged to a small child, but he did not see the remains of any children. My answer to this question after my research would be that like Víctor, other members of the rescue teams or journalist saw this doll and assumed it might belong to a child passenger.

In Spanish newspapers unlike the American press coverage, almost all the news of the C-141 crash were on the front page and most were accompanied by one or more photos. Also they described in more detail the rescue of the sole survivor by Antonio Beas and Víctor Martínez, and the recovery efforts of the remains of the deceased people of the crashed plane.

By contrast, none of the names of the crew or the passengers killed in this accident were published in any Spanish newspaper. Only the name of the sole survivor, First Lt. William Ray and his rescuers Antonio Beas and Víctor Martínez along with the others who helped transport the wounded to Antonio´s car were published.

One of the biggest controversies surrounding this accident is that in the Spanish newspapers contradictory versions regarding whether the plane was on fire before crashing. In some newspapers it was reported that some inhabitants of Valdeconcha (a village near Hueva) saw the plane on fire "with fire on board" before crashing. At present, witnesses interviewed in Valdeconcha, still ratifying that the aircraft had fire before crashing. Also according to some newspapers the testimony of one shepherd, Francisco Jimenez Sanchez is misunderstood, perpetrating in some media that the shepherd "saw the aircraft burning and then crashed" or "the plane was burning before falling" when what he actually said in an interview was "... I saw the plane coming rubbing the holm oaks, suddenly came out great flames and I thought the whole mountain was burning". In the interview of the shepherd, you can clearly understand the story that the shepherd did not see the plane flying afire, but rather the fire started after the plane's contact with the trees and then it crashed. Also in my interview with the sole survivor, First Lieutenant William Ray said there was nothing unusual during the descent till the moment of impact, statement that is also supported by transcripts of the conversations between the cockpit and the control tower.

DESERT SUN - Palm Springs, California August 29, 1973
Courtesy of Steven Cansler
Jet Crash Takes 24 Lives
Air Force Families Die En Route Home

MADRID (UPI) - A U.S. Air Force C141 jet transport plane crashed and burst into flames Tuesday night on a landing approach to the huge Torrejon airbase near Madrid.

The Air Force said today 24 of the 25 persons aboard died instantly in the fiery explosion. An Air Force spokesman said the sole survivor suffered a fractured leg and cuts, but had a good chance of living.

He identified him as the plane's navigator, 1st Lt. William H Ray, 25, of McGuire Air Force Base, N.J. The giant four-engine Starlifter cargo jet carried a crew of eight and 17 passengers.

According to the Spanish news agency Cifra, the <u>dead included three women and witnesses reported that there also were children aboard</u>. The news agency said the passengers were families of U.S. servicemen living abroad and that they were on their way home.

The Military Airlift Command (MAC) jet was en route from Athens to McGuire Air Force Base in New Jersey, with a stop planned at the giant Torrejon airbase 40 miles from Madrid. The plane went down in a grove of oak trees between the villages of Hueva and Pastrana, 22 miles from the Torrejon base, which is operated jointly by the air forces of Spain and the United States.

The Spanish Aviation Ministry said the <u>plane "lost contact with the Torrejon control tower at 10:50 p.m.</u> ... and crashed near Hueva, bursting into flames on impact." Witnesses said there was an explosion and reported wreckage strewn over a mile wide section of land Spanish police sealed off the crash site.

Air Force sources said an <u>U.S. F-4 Phantom jet fighter pilot flew over the stricken plane just before it went down for what was described as an emergency landing. "It seemed to land all right, but then bounced up and broke up, bursting into flames,"</u> the pilot was quoted as saying.

Spanish news reports said <u>the Survivor</u> was rescued from the wreckage of the plane's nose by villagers who arrived on the scene. "He <u>was apparently ejected from the aircraft on impact and suffered multiple fractures of the left leg and multiple contusions,"</u> the Air Force said.

24 Listed Killed On Air Force Jet

MADRID (AP) — A U.S. military cargo plane crashed 40 miles east of Madrid last night, and the Spanish Air Ministry said 24 of the 25 persons aboard were killed.

The C141 Starlifter jet was based at McGuire Air Force Base in New Jersey and was en route from Athens, Greece, to the U. S. Air Force base at Torrejon, 16 miles east of Madrid.

Spanish news agencies said the sole survivor was 1st Lt. William Ray, 25, a pilot, and that he had a broken leg. He was taken to the Torrejon base hospital, but his home address was not available.

Seventeen passengers and a crew of eight were reported aboard the plane, and there were unconfirmed reports that three women were among the passengers.

U.S. Air Force officials at Torrejon said they had no official word yet on casualties.

McGuire Air Force Base said it had no information on the plane.

The plane slammed into the ground about a mile outside the little town of Hueva as the craft was preparing to land at the joint Spanish-American base. Local police said none of the townspeople was affected.

The Air Ministry said the plane crashed after losing contact with the Torrejon control tower. It exploded when it hit the ground and burned, the ministry said.

U.S. and Spanish military authorities sealed off the crash site, and American rescue personnel and investigators were sifting through the wreckage today.

The Air Force said in addition to the people aboard, the plane was carrying nearly nine tons of cargo.

The Starlifter was attached to the Military Airlift Command. The Air Force said it was that command's first fatal accident since 1965.

NEW YORK TIMES - August 29, 1973

U.S. MILITARY JET CRASHES; 24 DEAD

Air Force Dependents Are Among Victims in Spain

MADRID, Aug. 29 (AP)—A United States military cargo jet plane with wives and children of American airmen among the 25 persons aboard crashed last night near Madrid, the United States Air Force said today. Only one crew member survived.

The plane, a C-141 StarLifter, struck the ground about 40 miles east of Madrid as it was approaching a United States-Spanish air base to land, the Air Force reported.

Spokesmen at the Torrejon base identified the lone sur-

The New York Times/Aug. 30, 1973

vivor as First Lieut. William H. Ray, 25 years old, of McGuire Air Force Base, N.J.

Doctors at the Torrejon base hospital said that Lieutenant Ray was in relatively stable condition 15 hours after the crash and was expected to recover.

He was one of the plane's navigators and was apparently ejected on impact, suffering multiple fractures in his left leg and multiple contusions on his body, Air Force spokesmen said.

Air Force officials said that they would identify the dead tomorrow after notifying next of kin. They said several wives and children of Air Force personnel were among the victims.

En Route from Athens

The Military Air Command jet, carrying nine tons of cargo, was on its way from Athens to the Torrejon air base, 16 miles east of Madrid. The craft was based at McGuire Air Force Base.

Wreckage was scattered over a two-mile stretch between the towns of Hueva and Pastrana. The towns were not affected. The area was cordoned off by the police and United States Air Force workers to facilitate rescue work.

The Air Force said the cause of the accident had not been determined. It said a committee of United States Air Force officers would be appointed to investigate.

Spanish news agencies said that rescue parties had not yet found the aircraft's black box, which records all cockpit conversations and instrument readings up to the moment of crash.

The agency reports said the plane had crashed against a small hill, careened about 600 yards and exploded on hitting the ground. Villagers reportedly heard cries from the plane, rushed to the wreckage and helped the single survivor to a Guadalajara clinic where he received first aid.

THE LEADER - September 6, 1973
Courtesy of Paul Hansen

THE LEADER, THURSDAY, SEPTEMBER 6, 1973   PAGE 13

Air Force Probes C-141 Tragedy

McGUIRE AFB • Military investigators continued their probe this week into the mysterious crash of a C-141 Starlifter jet aircraft from McGuire AFB which crashed on Aug. 28 near Madrid, Spain, killing 24 persons aboard.

The crash occured as the Starlifter, part of the 438th Military Airlift Wing based at McGuire AFB, attempted to land at Torrejon Air Base. There was only one survivor reported.

The massive four-engine jet, carrying 17 passengers and a crew of eight, was en route from Athens to Torrejon.

A military investigative committee has opened an inquest into the reasons for the tragedy. Eye witnesses reported the plane appeared to land safely enough though under emergency conditions but bounced, broke into pieces and finally burst into flames only seconds after ground impact.

The sole survivor was 1st Lt. William H. Ray who was apparently thrown clear of the wreckage. He was treated for a broken leg and multiple contusions.

Crew members killed were the pilot, Capt. Thomas R. Dietz, co-pilot Capt. Clinton C. Corbin, second co-pilot 1st Lt. William A. Kuhn, navigator, Maj. Frederich H. Lamers, flight engineers TSgt. Donald R. Wells and TSgt. Edward P. Babcock and loadmaster TSgt. Sidney N. Hillsman.

DECANO DE LA PRENSA DE LA TARDE - August 29, 1973
Courtesy of Zayda Beas

SE ESTRELLA UN AVION NORTEAMERICANO

En Hueva, cerca de la villa de Pastrana (Guadalajara), se estrelló un avión militar de transporte norteamericano que desde Atenas se dirigía a la base de Torrejón de Ardoz con 25 personas a bordo. Sólo hay un superviviente, el teniente piloto William Ray, que resultó con algunas fracturas. En la foto, los restos del avión, un C-141. (Cifra.)

24 MUERTOS Y UN SUPERVIVIENTE AL ESTRELLARSE UN AVION MILITAR NORTEAMERICANO CERCA DE PASTRANA

Venia de Atenas y traía a la base aérea de Torrejón material y personal de relevo ● Entre las víctimas figuran algunas mujeres ● El aparato se estrelló contra el suelo en las proximidades del

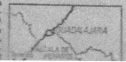

CHICAGO TRIBUNE - August 30, 1973

1 crewman survives crash

24 killed in Air Force jet

MADRID, Aug. 28 [AP]—A U. S. military cargo jet went down near Madrid with wives and children of American airmen among the 25 persons on board, the U. S. Air Force said today. Only one crewman survived the crash.

The C-141 StarLifter plummeted to the ground about 40 miles east of Madrid last night as it was approaching a U. S.-Spanish air base to land, the Air Force reported.

Spokesmen at the Torrejon base identified the lone survivor as 1st Lt. William H. Ray, 25, of McGuire Air Force Base, N. J.

DOCTORS AT the Torrejon base hospital said Ray was in relatively stable condition 15 hours after the crash and was expected to recover.

He was one of the plane's navigators and was apparently ejected on impact, suffering multiple fractures in his left leg and multiple cuts on the body, Air Force spokesmen said.

Air Force officials said they will identify the dead tomorrow after notifying next of kin. They said several wives and children of Air Force personnel were among the victims.

The Military Air Command jet, carrying nine tons of cargo, was on its way from Athens to the Torrejon air base 16 miles east of Madrid. It was based at McGuire Air Force Base.

WRECKAGE was scattered over a two-mile area between the towns of Hueva and Pastrana. The towns were not affected. The area was cordoned off by police and U. S. Air Force workers to facilitate rescue work.

The Air Force said the cause of the accident has not been determined. They added that a committee of U. S. Air Force officers would be appointed to investigate it.

Spanish news agencies said rescue parties had not yet found the aircraft's black box, which records all cockpit conversations and instrument readings up to the moment of crash.

The agency reports said the cargo jet crashed against a small hill, careened about 600 yards, and exploded.

Villagers reportedly heard cries from the plane, rushed to the wreckage, and helped the single survivor to a Guadalajara clinic where he received first aid.

in fashion for fall...

DETROIT FREE PRESS - August 30, 1973
Courtesy of William H. (Bill) Ray

AP Photo

Transport jet crash left nothing but a pile of wreckage

U.S. Jet Crashes in Spain; 24 Are Killed, One Survives

MADRID—(UPI)—A four-engine jet transport of the United States Military Airlift Command crashed and burned when landing at Torrejon Air Base near Madrid, killing all but one of the 25 persons aboard, the Air Force said Wednesday.

Witnesses reported that several women and children were among the dead. Spanish news reports said the plane was carrying dependents of servicemen stationed overseas.

The Air Force said the plane carried 17 passengers and eight crew members and almost nine tons of cargo.

The survivor, First Lt. William H. Ray, 25, of McGuire Air Force Base, N.J., was thrown clear on impact. He suffered multiple fractures of his left leg and contusions.

He was reported in "relatively stable condition."

The C-141 Starlifter, on a flight from Athens to McGuire via Madrid, crashed Tuesday night 22 miles from Torrejon near the village of Huera in a flat area dotted with oak and olive trees. Wreckage was strewn more than a mile.

Air Force sources quoted a U.S. F-4 Phantom jet fighter pilot who flew over the plane's path as saying, "It seemed to land all right, but then bounced up and broke up, bursting into flames."

The Spanish Air Ministry said radio contact between the plane and the Torrejon control tower broke off at 10:50 p.m. Neither U.S. nor Spanish air force authorities — who jointly operate the Torrejon base — gave any indication of what might have caused the crash or whether the plane sent out distress signals.

Bodies of 24 Killed in Crash In Spain to Be Flown to U.S.

MADRID, Aug. 30 (AP) — The bodies of 24 Americans killed in the crash of a United States Air Force cargo jet have been brought to the Torrejon air base to be flown to the United States.

The dead include wives and children of Air Force personnel, officials said.

The lone survivor, First Lieut. William H. Ray, 25 years old, of McGuire Air Force Base in New Jersey, who is in the hospital at the base east of Madrid, was a navigator of the plane and apparently was ejected when the C-141 jet crashed Tuesday night 40 miles east of Madrid.

McGUIRE AIR FORCE BASE, N. J., Aug. 30 (AP)—The Air Force today released the names of some of the 24 persons killed in the crash. They included First Lieut. William A. Kuhn, co-pilot, 24, of Northport, L. I.

VÍCTOR MARTÍNEZ VIANA
CORREPONSAL DE NUEVA ALCARRIA EN HUEVA

El accidente de avión de Hueva

El día 28 de agosto de año 1973 ocurrió un accidente aéreo, dejando 24 muertos de los 25 ocupantes dicho avión. Cuarenta años se han cumplido del fatídico accidente aéreo que horrorizó a la Villa de Hueva (Guadalajara) en la noche de aquel 28 de agosto. Un avión de las fuerzas aéreas de Estados Unidos se estrelló en el paraje conocido como B de Majadahonda o El Serrano. Llevaba 25 personas, entre tripulación y pasajeros, entre ellos algún niño, muriendo en el acto, salvo un superviviente, que hoy vive, gracias a la actuación de los vecinos de dicha localidad. El teniente William H. Ray, único superviviente del accidente, fue llevado e internado en primer lugar en la Residencia de la Seguridad Social en Guadalajara.

El modelo del avión era un C-141, de las fuerzas Aéreas Americanas, que venía desde Atenas a Nueva Jersey, con escala en la Base de Torrejón de Ardoz. Llevaba 17 pasajeros, ocho tripulantes y cerca de 9 toneladas de carga general. El artefacto no pudo hacer dicha escala, porque se estrelló unos metros antes de llegar a la población de Hueva. Se llevaron la caja negra, pero nunca se supo de ella.

Entre las 22.45 a las 23.00 horas de dicho día, todos los vecinos oímos una gran explosión, quedando la localidad iluminada. La villa completa de chicos y de mayores y algún enfermo, todos alarmados, nos lanzamos al lugar donde se veían las grandes llamas de dicho avión. Las primeras personas en acudir al lugar del accidente fuimos los vecinos Antonio Beas Pérez de Tudela Enviz y Víctor Martínez Viana, casados con dos hijas de la localidad. Al llegar al sitio del fuego, los dos cuñados, vimos dos zonas que ardían mucho. Antonio marchó a una de ellas y Víctor a la otra, quedando en llamarnos el uno al otro. Yo llamé muchas veces a Antonio, y después de varias vueltas por la zona incendiada y al no ver nada que se moviese, ya que todo estaba en llamas, vimos que allí se movía algo o alguien. Comprobamos que había una persona y Antonio empezó a sacarla. Entre los dos le sacamos, hasta que acudió más gente. Las piernas las llevaba rotas, a mí me relevaron a medio camino, Milagros Serrano, Federico Plaza Alcaide e Isidro Sáez. Una vez en el coche, que estaba

Homenaje a los vecinos de Hueva que participaron en el rescate de las víctimas del avión siniestrado.

distante del avión incendiado, casi todo el pueblo ya se encontraba en el monte. Caminamos hacia Guadalajara en su coche, un Seat Blanco. Paramos en el médico de Horche, lo vio y nos recomendó que siguiésemos a la Residencia de Guadalajara.

Al llegar a la Residencia de Guadalajara, ya estaba el equipo de urgencia esperándonos. Una vez en el Residencia de la Seguridad Social, se llevaron enseguida al herido a urgencias, pero mi cuñado Antonio se desmayó y tuvimos que atenderle también. Después de estar con él cinco horas en la Residencia, nos marchamos a Hueva. Yo casi no podía conducir, ya que tres días antes tuve un accidente de coche en la carretera de Tendilla, pero saqué fuerzas y llegamos a Hueva. Tardamos en llegar casi una hora y media.

Esa noche fui al monte donde se estrelló el avión. La policía militar americana no dejaba pasar a nadie a la zona incendiada ni tampoco a mí. Me entero y oigo que los primeros auxilios que salieron desde la base de Torrejón se fueron a Ocaña. Todas las fuerzas españolas y equipos de seguridad y salvamento español llegaron antes donde el accidente que los americanos. Yo esa noche me mosqueé y me pareció mal que no necesitaran nuestra ayuda.

El embajador americano, el gobernador civil de la provincia, militares del Ministerio del Aire Español y de la Base de Torrejón, el día 20 de octubre del 1973 tributaron un gran homenaje a todo el pueblo, y muy en especial a Antonio Beas Pérez de Tudela Enviz y Víctor Martínez Viana, con sendos diplomas. También entregaron un pergamino al Ayuntamiento, que recogió el alcalde, en nombre de la villa de Hueva, de manos del embajador de los EE. UU. Lo que sí tengo claro es que todo el pueblo de la villa de Hueva salvamos la vida a un semejante y volveríamos hacer lo mismo otras veces si llegase la ocasión. Por 60 segundos nos salvamos todos los vecinos de morir carbonizados. Por dos motivos, o el piloto vio el peligro y se estrelló contra el suelo o un milagro, yo creo que fue un milagro. Si es así le damos las gracias al piloto y si es un milagro, quizás debamos este milagro al padre franciscano Fray Félix Gómez-Pinto Piñero, hoy beato y muy querido por las gentes de Hueva. De una forma o de otra, damos las gracias por seguir contando este hecho que marcó la historia de nuestra Villa de Hueva, en plena Alcarria, provincia de Guadalajara, España.

SOLO UN SUPERVIVIENTE

Guadalajara: SE ESTRELLA UN AVION NORTEAMERICANO DE TRANSPORTE CON VEINTICINCO PERSONAS A BORDO

Guadalajara, 29. (Resumen de Agencias y de nuestro corresponsal, Luis MONJE CIRUELO.) — Veinticuatro muertos y un superviviente es el balance del accidente de aviación ocurrido a las 10.45 de la pasada noche en el término de Hueva, a unos 5 kilómetros de Pastrana. Un avión C-141 «Starlifter C-141», que volaba desde Atenas a Torrejón de Ardoz en ruta hacia su base de McGuire, Nueva Jersey, se estrelló en la meseta alcarreña, a unos 2 kilómetros del pueblecito de Hueva, de unos 250 habitantes. Transportaba el aparato 17 pasajeros, entre ellos varias mujeres, 8 tripulantes y 8,8 toneladas de carga general. Milagrosamente ha sobrevivido a la catástrofe el primer teniente piloto, Willians Ray, de 25 años, quien sufrió solamente fractura abierta de tibia y peroné. Después de curado en la Residencia Sanitaria de la Seguridad Social de Guadalajara, fue trasladado al Hospital Militar de la base de Torrejón. Recogieron al herido, guiados en la oscuridad de la noche por sus lamentos, los primeros vecinos de Hueva que llegaron, apenas media hora después, al lugar del accidente.

Se ignoran las causas del siniestro.

(Continúa en la página siguiente)

24 muertos al estrellarse un «starlifter» de las Fuerzas de los Estados Unidos en la provincia de Guadalajara

Se salvó milagrosamente el primer teniente piloto, que sufre diversas heridas y fue quien pidió auxilio

GUADALAJARA, 29 (Pyresa).—Dos kilómetros de campo sembrados de chatarra y 24 personas muertas —entre ellas tres mujeres y por lo menos un niño—, sufre fractura de la pierna izquierda y rasponazos en la cara, es el balance del accidente sufrido por un avión «C-141» «starlifter», de las fuerzas aéreas estadounidenses, a las 22'45 horas de ayer, en las cercanías de Hueva, pedanía de Pastrana (Guadalajara).

Los vecinos de Hueva se personaron inmediatamente en el lugar del suceso, para prestar ayuda a las víctimas. D. Antonio Byas Pérez de Tudela fue el primero en descubrir al primer teniente piloto del avión siniestrado, William Ray, que pedía socorro. Acompañaba al señor Byas su cuñado, D. Víctor Martínez, a quien le pareció escuchar gritos de auxilio.

Los vecinos de Hueva apagaron las llamas que prendían en algunos cuerpos, y comprobaron que no existían más supervivientes que el teniente Ray, quien reiteradamente solicitaba que se le trasladase a Torrejón de Ardoz. Los señores Byas y Martínez lo llevaron, en el coche del primero, hasta Horche, en donde el médico prescribió su traslado a Guadalajara, y el mismo se dirigió a Hueva para prestar su ayuda en el lugar de la catástrofe.

En Guadalajara recibió el teniente Ray la necesaria asistencia médica, y esta mañana, cuando iba a ser trasladado a Torrejón de Ardoz, abrazó emocionadamente a la primera persona que le prestó ayuda, el Sr. Byas, que desde entonces sufre una crisis nerviosa, hasta el punto de que el juez del accidente,

Pasa a la pág. 10

24 MUERTOS AL ESTRELLARSE...

Viene de la primera

Comandante Espinosa, ha tenido que posponer su interrogatorio por no encontrarse en condiciones de prestar declaración.

La única persona que vió el aparato antes de estrellarse es el pastor Francisco Giménez Sánchez, quien se extrañó de que tuviese fijas las luces de posición —dos rojas y una verde— y de que volara demasiado bajo, aunque no pudo precisar si su declaración si el aparato llevaba fuera el tren de aterrizaje, como parece pudo ocurrir por las huellas dejadas en el monte de El Encinar, en el paraje denominado Alto de Valdecosa. El señor Jiménez Sánchez, no perdió de vista el avión y lo vió chocar contra el suelo, rebotar y volver a caer un kilómetro más allá. Asegura que el avión ardía antes de caer, y que la segunda explosión fue mucho más violenta que la primera.

Inmediatamente después de producirse el accidente, se personaron en el lugar de la catástrofe fuerzas de la Guardia Civil. Un equipo de treinta personas, entre sanitarios, policía del ejército de los Estados Unidos, de guarnición en la base conjunta de Torrejón de Ardoz, salió a media noche de la base para hacerse cargo de los trabajos de rescate a las dos de la madrugada. Al amanecer se inició el acopio de material que conduciría a conocer las causas del siniestro y la recogida de objetos personales de las víctimas. El levantamiento de cadáveres se hizo a partir de las 13'30 y hasta las 14'30 horas de hoy.

Esta mañana inspeccionaron el lugar el General de División D. Salvador Feliices, Jefe de las fuerzas estadounidenses de la base de Torrejón de Ardoz; Gobernador Civil y Jefe Provincial del Movimiento, accidental, de Guadalajara, y el Gobernador Militar de dicha provincia, entre otras autoridades. Se rumorea que inspeccionará la catástrofe un general estadounidense enviado especialmente desde Los Angeles (California).

El «C-141» «Starlifter» mide 48 metros de largo y 119 metros de alto. Tiene una velocidad de crucero de quinientas millas por hora y alcanzan un techo de 12.300 metros. Puede transportar unos 158.000 kilos además de 154 soldados con su equipo.

El último accidente con víctimas que sufrió el comando estadounidense encargado de este tipo de servicios de transporte de personal se registró en 1965. Desde entonces, en este tipo de aparatos el ejército de los Estados Unidos ha realizado seis millones de horas de vuelo sin pérdidas humanas.

WALTON ...TIONAL
...VICES, S. A. E.
...guientes especialidades Torrevieja a convenir. Teléf. 222686.

152

Death Rode C-141, But McGuire Eight Never Knew Fear

By JIM GALLAGHER
And
JOHN KATZENBACH
Staff Writers

McGUIRE AFB — They never worried much about death.

Like other men drive to work in the morning, the eight crewmen of the C-141 routinely climbed into the giant plane and flew to all parts of the world.

IT IS HARD TO CHARACTERIZE the men who flew the ill-fated transport. Two were bachelors, six were family men. Some came to the Air Force after college, others worked up through the ranks.

But at 3:19 p.m. Sunday they were part of a team, each with a carefully defined job to do, flying out of McGuire Air Force Base to Athens, Greece, then return. Tuesday evening seven of them were dead in the twisted wreckage of their plane, littering the burnt Spanish countryside near Torrejon. One survived.

The crash also claimed the lives of seventeen passengers — military men and their dependents from all over the United States.

The lone survivor, Lt. William R. Ray, 25, a navigator, of Falcon Courts, McGuire, was thrown clear of the plane when it plunged to earth. He is in a Spanish hospital in good condition with multiple leg fractures.

THE LOADMASTER

Technical Sgt. Sidney Hillsman of 205 Carlisle Avenue, Yardville, never discussed his work with his family.

The citation that went with his Distinguished Flying Cross and Cluster Air Medal said he showed "personal bravery" flying "extremely hazardous missions through adverse weather with the threat of enemy ground fire and attack."

But, through all his letters from Vietnam, he never mentioned danger.

"When he would write to me, it would be about how he missed me and the children," said his wife Lois. "He never wrote me to say he didn't like it there. If his job was hazardous, he never let me know."

SGT. HILLSMAN An Air Force friend remembers him as "quiet

and efficient," a "family man" who liked children and coached the base Little League team.

He leaves his wife and three children — Cynthia, 12; Rodney, 10, and Lisa, 6.

THE PILOT

The pilot, Capt. Thomas R. Dietz, lived with his wife at McGuire, but grew up in Milwaukee, Wis. He is remembered by his father, Henry, as "a born leader." He was a Cub Scout, an Eagle Scout and president of his Explorer troop.

His father described him as a "real go-getter" who never really knew failure.

He worked hard at everything — church choir, student government at St. Olaf's College in Northfield, Minn., the track team and playing the piano. His father said Capt. Dietz paid for all his expenses through college, graduating in 1969, then entering the Air Force.

In June, Capt. Dietz' **CAPT. DIETZ** parents visited him at McGuire. The elder Dietz remembers being taken up in a small Cessna after a day being shown through the base, and the C-141 his son flew. It was, he said, like seeing his son's future from the cockpit of the small craft, as they slowly circled the area.

THE FIRST CO-PILOT

The first co-pilot, Capt. Clinton C. Corbin of 75-A Millside Manor Apartments, Delran, came from a military family — his father was a retired Air Force pilot. Capt. Corbin in early life developed a love of the outdoors.

Capt. Corbin was not a hunter, though, his father explained. Once, as a boy, he and a friend had shot a bird, and the act had made him sick. His father said he then decided never to hunt again.

After graduating from Southwest Texas State in 1969 and faced with a military obligation, Corbin **CAPT. CORBIN** joined the Air Force. "He understood the service."

his father said.

And he loved to fly, his father added. At

(Continued on Page 3, Col. 5)

Death Rode C-141, But McGuire Eight Never Knew Fear

(Continued from Page 1)

the time of the last flight, he was considering buying his own plane. But, his father said, the Air Force wasn't going to be Capt. Corbin's career.

"We thought he probably would become a teacher," he said. His son, he said, liked people, and wanted to work with them.

The Second Co-pilot

The second co-pilot, 1st Lt. william A. Kuhn, of Sherwood Village Apartments, Mount Holly, also loved to fly. His father said he first became interested in flying before joining the Air Force Reserve Officer Training Program at Notre Dame.

His father said he was a "studious" man who did everything with a quiet intensity. A good athlete, he was on the wrestling team at Notre Dame.

LT. KUHN

His father remembers he enjoyed working on the family's summer house in upstate New York. A few weeks ago, he went there while on leave to paint the garage. He had planned to finish the job when he returned.

"He had direction," his father said. Lt. Kuhn, his father added was always "serious," but with a sense of humor. He grew up on Long Island and all his life "he would always listen to all sides of a question," then decide what was right, and go ahead, his father recalled.

The Navigators

Maj. Friedrick H. Lamers, 40, was a man who liked music and photography.

A 15-year Air Force veteran, he was one of the first to volunteer for combat when the Indochina War began to intensify in 1964. There, he earned the Air Medal navigating gunships.

MAJ. LAMERS

He returned from his last combat tour this Summer.

"There were times when I thought he was gone too much," said his wife, Ruth. "But he was very dedicated.

"He was a good husband, a good father, a very honest man."

His wife and two children, Carla, 14, and Steven, 9, live at the Sherwood Village Apartments, Mount Holly.

First Flight Engineer

Tech. Sgt. Donald R. Wells, 40, was "the jovial type — a pleasure to be around."

As opposed to many of the crewmen, who were described as quiet men, Sargeant Wells was happy-go-lucky, a friend remembers. "He was always friendly and a pleasure to be around."

Wells' wife and two boys live at 4227F Falcon Courts, McGuire AFB.

SGT. WELLS

Second Flight Engineer

Tech. Sgt. Edward P. Babcock was the "quiet type, not too talkative and very calm," according to an Air Force co-worker.

A flight engineer, he spent most of his free time with his wife and three children at Dover AFB, Dela.

SGT. BABCOCK

At the base last night, one man who had flown with all the dead crewmen talked about the dangers in flying. No one worried, he said. "Maybe a new man might worry, but they get used to it."

"They know things like this could happen, but it doesn't worry you because it's so rare on an aircraft like this C141.

"You just figure you're doing a helluva job."

LA CATASTROFE AEREA DE GUADALAJARA
Pudo intentar un aterrizaje de emergencia

Las declaraciones del superviviente, navegante del aparato, decisivas para aclarar las causas

NADA nuevo sobre la catastrofe aérea de Hueva, en la provincia de Guadalajara, en la que perecieron 24 personas, al estrellarse un avión de transporte norteamericano. Oficialmente, tan sólo se ha dado a conocer una nota oficial del Ministerio español del Aire, en la que se habla de que a bordo del avión viajaban «unas veinticinco personas». La Embajada de los Estados Unidos en Madrid se limitó a confirmar el accidente. Por su parte, la base aérea de Torrejón de Ardoz, en cuyo aeropuerto iba a tomar tierra el avión siniestrado, no ha publicado comunicado alguno. Sin embargo, se sabe que probablemente hoy se dará a conocer la lista de víctimas, una vez que ha sido comunicada la noticia a los familiares de las mismas. Como ya informamos ayer, uno de los 25 ocupantes del avión se salvó milagrosamente, sufriendo solamente algunas fracturas y erosiones.

EL superviviente de la catastrofe que, al parecer, salió despedido del aparato al chocar éste contra el suelo es un teniente de las Fuerzas Aéreas de los Estados Unidos. Se trata del teniente Williams H. Ray, con destino en Nueva Jersey y que viajaba en el avión en calidad de «navegator» o encargado de la navegación. El teniente Ray, después de ser asistido en el hospital de Guadalajara, quedó internado en el de la base aérea de Torrejón de Ardoz, donde a mediodía de ayer recibió la visita del vecino de Hueva (Guadalajara), que le recogió y le trasladó en su coche hasta el primer centro sanitario. Por cierto, este hombre, después de poner a salvo al teniente Ray, sufrió una crisis nerviosa, que incluso le llegó a impedir prestar declaración ante el juez militar que instruye el sumario por la catastrofe.

Respecto a la investigación, según fuentes generalmente bien informadas, se asegura que tomará parte en ella, en calidad de asistente de las autoridades españolas —está claro que en territorio español ocurrió el siniestro— un general de las U. S. A. F. que tendrá [...]

niente Ray, determinarán las causas exactas del accidente.

Hasta el momento, lo único que se sabe es que el avión perdió contacto con la torre de control de la base de Torrejón segundos antes de estrellarse. No ha trascendido si en su última conversación el piloto comunicó a la torre que tuviera dificultades en el aparato o si éstas surgieron tan repentinas como irremediablemente. Sin embargo, el hecho de que los vecinos de Hueva coinciden en afirmar que el avión iba muy bajo y el lugar donde se estrelló —una gran planicie— pueden hacer pensar en que el piloto, perdido ya el control con tierra, intentó un aterrizaje de emergencia, ya que incluso parece ser que existen rodadas del tren de aterrizaje en el lugar del accidente.

Respecto al tipo de aparato siniestrado es quizá uno de los más seguros con los que cuentan las Fuerzas Aéreas de los Estados Unidos. El C-141 Starlifter, que está considerado como el más moderno avión de carga operativo de las Fuerzas Aéreas norteamericanas. Respecto a la seguridad del aparato bastará decir que voló por primera vez en diciembre de 1963, entrando en servicio en 1965, año en que comenzó a utilizarse en la guerra del Vietnam. Fue precisamente en 1965 cuando se accidentó un aparato de este tipo y desde entonces hasta el accidente de Guadalajara no volvió a protagonizar un siniestro un C-141. En total, las 200 unidades construidas hasta el momento llevan voladas un total de casi siete millones de horas. Con una velocidad máxima de crucero de 908 kilómetros por hora, puede llevar 154 soldados equipados, 127 paracaidistas, 80 camillas con los sanitarios adecuados o bien una carga de 42.680 kilos.

De cualquier forma, todo hace pensar que la investigación se verá muy simplificada, pues se cuenta con un superviviente que, además, era tripulante del aparato y directamente relacionado con la conducción del mismo. Parece ser que todavía no ha sido hallada la «caja negra» que, junto con el relato del te-

Manuel E. MARLASCA

Desde 1965 no tenía ningún accidente un avión de este tipo, considerado como el más seguro de las U. S. A. F.

HUEVA

Cuarenta años esperando respuestas

El 28 de agosto de 1973 un accidente aéreo dejó 24 muertos y un único superviviente

Cuarenta años se cumplieron el miércoles del fatídico accidente aéreo que horrorizó a la localidad de Hueva en la noche de aquel día 28 de agosto. Un avión de la Fuerzas Aéreas Estadounidenses se estrellaba en el paraje conocido como Bajón de Majahonda. Veinticuatro personas, entre tripulación y pasajeros, murieron en el acto y sólo quedó un superviviente, que vivió gracias a la rápida actuación de los vecinos de la localidad. Concretamente, Víctor Martínez Viana y Antonio Beas Pérez, que por primera vez hablan sobre los sucedido. El teniente William Ray fue internado en Guadalajara y luego en Torrejón. Mucha incógnitas rodean el suceso y los "héroes" de Hueva esperan respuestas.

NUEVA
VÍCTOR MARTÍNEZ VIANA

La villa de Hueva, una vez más recuerda el triste accidente de avión, ocurrido el día 28 de agosto del año 1973, donde fallecieron 24 de las 25 personas que viajaban en dicho avión, modelo C_141, de las Fuerzas Aéreas Americanas Despegando en Azores con destino a New Jersey y con escala en la base de Torrejón. El artefacto no hizo tal escala porque se estrelló en el término del serrano en Hueva (Guadalajara) a poca distancia de la villa.

Éstas son mis primeras declaraciones completas que realizo sobre dicho accidente y Nueva Alcarria las recoge en primicia. Es todo lo que sigo pensando desde aquel fatídico día.

Entre las 22.45 a las 23 horas de dicho día, todos los vecinos oímos una gran explosión, quedando toda la localidad iluminada. La población, tanto chicos, mayores y grandes y algún enfermo, alarmados, nos lanzamos al lugar de donde se veía las grandes llamas y con tu alcalde también. De dicho accidente se ocupó toda la prensa, provincial, nacional y parte del extranjero.

Las primeras personas en llegar al lugar del accidente fueron los vecinos, Antonio Beas Pérez de Tudela Enviz y Víctor Martínez Viana–yo mismo–consortes de dos hermanas hijas del lugar. Al llegar al fuego, los dos cuñados vimos dos zonas incendiadas. Antonio se fue a una y yo a la otra y quedamos en llamarnos el uno al otro. Llamé muchas veces a Antonio, y después de un gran rato dando vueltas en la zona incendiada y al no ver nada que se moviese, todo estaba en llamas, me marché a ver a Antonio, que ya me llamaba, y me decía que allí se movía alguien. Efectivamente, le ayudé a vaciarlo. Entre los dos, por el monte, de noche, y con las piernas rotas del herido colgando, lo llevamos hasta el coche. Era un Seat 124 blanco. Hacia nosotros acudían el resto de vecinos, como Milagros Serrano, Federico Plaza, alcalde, Isidro Sáez. Nos echaron una mano hasta llegar al vehículo, que estaba distante del avión incendiado. Después acudieron muchas personas, yo creo que casi todo el pueblo.

Desde el coche y conduciendo mi cuñado Antonio, nos fuéramos a todo para a Guadalajara. Yo iba en la parte trasera con el herido, cogiéndole las manos, el cuerpo y dándole ánimo. Recuerdo que decía, ¿Se nos muere, Antonio?, ¿qué no se nos muera, madre mía!, repetía yo en esta gran chico de sangre y con la piernas que se trocían por estar partidas. Tuvo que sufrir mucho el teniente W.H.Ray. No dejaba de repetir, "Antonio!", "Antonio!", "madre mía". No dećia otra cosa en todo el viaje. Durante el trayecto a Guadalajara, paramos en el médico de Horche y nos recomendó seguir a Guadalajara, ya que según iba el herido no podía hacer casi nada. Una vez en el mismo Hospital de Guadalajara, ya estaba el equipo de Urgencias esperando. (En el monte, le dije a Federico, el alcalde, que llamase otra vez al Gobierno Civil primero y después al hospital).

Una vez en el hospital, se llevaron enseguida al herido, que era el teniente W.W.Ray, pero mi cuñado Antonio se destrayó y hubo que atenderle también. Después de estar con el cuarto o cinco horas en el hospital, sólos, nos marchamos a Hueva.

Yo esa noche no podía conducir, ya que días antes tuve un accidente de coche en Tendilla pero saqué fuerzas y llegamos a Hueva. Tardamos casi hora y media. Mi cuñado tardó en reponerse más de un mes. No hicimos ninguna declaración, a pesar de que toda la prensa estaba detrás de nosotros aquellos días... Hasta hoy.

Demasiadas preguntas

Yo subí al monte, donde se estrelló el avión era misma madrugada. La Policía Militar no me dejaba pasar a la zona incendiada ¿Después de lo que había pasado yo, pero el sargento de Pastrana de la Guardia Civil, les dijo quién era y pasé. Recuerdo que me presentaron a mucha gente, en especial militares y algún paisano, otros me preguntaron por el accidente como alguna que otra pregunta a nivel oficial de la que yo me percaté. Me entero que los auxilios primeros que salieron de Torrejón, se largaron hacia Ocaña. Todas las fuerzas españolas y equipos de seguridad y salvamento llegaron antes que los americanos a Hueva. Pero no dejaron que ningún servicio español diese rescate les ayudasen. Yo esa noche me mosquee y me pareció mal que no necesitaran nuestra ayuda.

Me pregunto muchas veces, ya que a mí jamás me han dado ninguna versión oficial del accidente y creo que me la merezco, si el avión repostaba en Torrejón, ¿cómo es que hubo tanto fuego en las dos zonas que se dividió el avión? Si aun los depósitos estaban vacíos, según el yo, ¿Por qué hubo un gran resplandor? Corrieron en dejar limpio todo rápidamente. Nada más hubo policía americana.

El teniente W.W.Ray, fue rápidamente trasladado a Torrejón desde el hospital de Guadalajara. Se temió por algún contagio? Me gustaría tener respuestas sobre el accidente. Era un avión muy seguro para tener accidentes.

El teniente W.Ray tan solo me escribió tres cartas desde EE.UU., las mismas que yo le conteste. El año 79, realicé un viaje a EE.UU, estuve en Nueva Jersey, en una misión oficial, y el Pentágono no lo pudo localizar.

Para mí, todo lo que rodea a este accidente sigue siendo muy raro. Ahora parece que han escrito un libro, que por cierto en cuanto a los sucesos que acontecieron esa noche en Hueva ... Es lamentable su contenido. No sé quién o quienes informaron al escritor, y a qué viene ahora querer remover lo ocurrido aquella larga noche, al menos para mí. También aparecen periodistas por Hueva, no se quiénes han dado la versión que pone el libro, lo único que se que no es la real. Yo soy localizable y jamás nadie me ha preguntado, ni estando en Hueva, y soy uno de los que vivieron más el accidente del avión. También visitaron al teniente en Torrejón Antonio Beas y Víctor Martínez Viana.

Debo manifestar que el Ayuntamiento de Hueva, siendo alcalde Federico Plaza, fue el que puso la lápida y la pagó, recordando dicho accidente y en memoria de todos los fallecidos que fueron 24 y pudieron ser 25.

Los americanos ya su embajador, el gobernador civil y autoridades, el día 20 de octubre del año 1973, tributaron un homenaje, a Antonio Beas y Víctor Martínez Viana, con sendos diplomas en prueba de agradecimiento y un pergamino al Ayuntamiento que fue recibido por el alcalde, en nombre de la villa de Hueva. El teniente W.Ray nos regaló un reloj a cada uno.

Yo, al menos, no he necesitado ni he pedido ni he recibido nunca nada por hacer un bien a un semejante y salvarle la vida junto a la gente de Hueva. Hoy, yo al menos, no tengo contacto con dicho teniente, ni jamás la Embajada se ha dignado en escribir para el aniversario algunas que otras letras.

Lo que sí tengo claro es que todo el pueblo de Hueva salvamos la vida a un semejante, y volveríamos a hacer lo mismo otra vez. Por setenta segundos nos salvamos los vecinos, o el piloto vio el peligro e hizo estrellar el avión contra el suelo. Si es así yo le doy las gracias, para que podamos seguir contando este hecho que ha marcado la historia de Hueva.

Imagen publicada en Nueva Alcarria del artefacto estrellado.

El suceso ocupó la portada de Nueva Alcarria en 1973.

Autoridades civiles y militares en la entrega del diploma a Víctor Martínez.

Tomando una copa en el bar Celaya de Hueva.

El superviviente americano del accidente aéreo regresa en fiestas

El teniente William Ray visitó la villa 42 años después

HUEVA
VÍCTOR MARTÍNEZ VIANA

Con una inmensa alegría de todo corazón y después de 42 años, nos volvemos a ver, tanto el salvado como los salvadores del brutal accidente ocurrido en nuestra villa de Hueva (Guadalajara) el día 28 de agosto del año 1973, donde ese día un avión americano de las Fuerzas Armadas, al volar por nuestro espacio aéreo de Hueva, se estrelló, dirección a la base de Torrejón de Ardoz en Madrid. Su ruta era, desde Atenas a Nueva Yersi U.S.A.

En esas fechas, toda la prensa de España se hizo eco del desgraciado accidente de aviación. Sus protagonistas esa noche fueron toda la población de Hueva, había que intentar salvar a toda la gente, pero solo pudimos salvar al teniente William H. Ray, siendo sus salvadores directos Antonio Beas Pérez de Tudela Enviz y Víctor Martínez Viana, luego también, acudieron Federico, Milagros, Isidro y demás personas.

Pues bien estos días de fiestas patronales tuvimos la suerte de contar con la presencia del 'americano', como le llamaba la gente a su paso por las calles del pueblo. Con qué cariño ha sido saludado William, Hueva no olvida aquella noche trágica. Me decía que devolviese los saludos y gracias a todos. Para mí ha sido un placer pasear por las calles de Hueva, con el 'americano'– que sonaba muy bien–.

Después de 42 años sin vernos, ha sido un gran honor el ser recibido, tanto para nosotros como para nuestra familia por William Ray en estos días de fiestas en la villa. Cuando ocurrió el accidente tenía 26 años, hoy regresa con 68 años al lugar de los hechos desde el que hoy lo puede contar gracias a Dios

Se le nota que no quiere saber nada de recuerdos de aquel día

Superviviente y salvadores al poco del accidente.

El teniente Ray recibió el libro del 75 Aniversario de Nueva Alcarria donde aparece la retrospectiva de la tragedia áerea

tan desgraciado del accidente. Se lamenta de no haber podido compartir con su esposa estos momentos, pero no podía viajar con él. Sí que nos mandó recuerdos de su parte.

Que dos días maravillosos que he pasado con William. (Guillermo) en Hueva, el podernos ver de tú a tú, después de 42 años y de 40 sin saber nada de nada el uno del otro. Para mí también es un orgullo que un semejante se acuerde tanto de mi como de mi familia. Nos intercambiamos regalos, yo entre ellos el libro de los 75 años del aniversario de **Nueva Alcarria**, donde está un articulo mío precisamente sobre el accidente del avión de ese día.

Quiero hacer mención especial y un ruego, que cuando se escriba un libro sobre dicho accidente, consulten a las fuentes reales en sus personas. Que no digan una sarta de mentiras sobre dicho accidente. Ahora hay uno, que no sé de donde lo han sacado las fuentes de información para escribirlo.

Debo de agradecer a José Manuel Pascual, la persona que localizó al 'americano' en EE.UU por Internet por que en estos días yo al menos he gozado con su presencia. Gracias Chasquita. Yo lo intenté cuando visité EE.UU, el año 1979, pero no se le localizó, y sin embargo desde Hueva, si. Lo que es la ciencia.

En nombre de toda la familia, te deseamos mucha suerte como a tu familia Guillermo. Sabes que seguimos apreciándote de todo corazón, y que estés restablecido del accidente de aquella noche en Hueva. Es bonito que existan estos lazos de amistad entre las personas. La nuestra cuenta con ella. Hasta siempre William (Guillermo).

PHOTOS

PHOTOS FROM THE CRASH SITE:

160

161

PHOTOS FROM HUEVA MEMORIAL OCTOBER 20, 1973:

Antonio, Bill, Federico, Milagros and Víctor

SLIDES FOUND AT THE CRASH SITE:

NAVY DIVING OFFICER´S PIN FROM CHRIS KATSETOS
FOUND AT THE CRASH SITE:

VISIT TO THE CRASH SITE:

Antonio Beas with Gustavo

REMAINS OF THE AIRCRAFT FOUND AT THE CRASH SITE
APRIL 12, 2016:

CARPETA DOSIER INVESTIGATION TEAM:

Cristian, Gustavo and Rubén
For any comments or suggestions,
you can write to the writer´s email:
gustavodomenech1976@hotmail.com

HUEVA DEATH CERTIFICATES

L 003885   P 012

Número 19

REGISTRO CIVIL DE _Hueva_

DATOS DE IDENTIDAD DEL DIFUNTO: varón

Nombre   FRIADRICH H.

Primer apellido   LAMARS

Segundo apellido

hija de ████████   y de ████████

Estado   nacionalidad   USA

Nacido el día   ocho   de   agosto

de   mil novecientos treinta y dos

en   (NEADHERST (Inglaterra)

Inscrito al tomo   ████████

Domicilio último   ████████

DEFUNCIÓN: Hora   día   veintiocho

de   agosto   de   mil novecientos setenta

Lugar   término municipal de Hueva (Guadalajara)

Causa   Accidente del avión C-141 de las F.A. norteamericanas

El enterramiento será en   Estados Unidos de América

DECLARACIÓN DE D.

En su calidad de

Domicilio

Comprobación: Médico D.

Colegiado núm.   número del parte

OTROS TÍTULOS O DATOS

ENCARGADO D.   Leonardo Pérez López

SECRETARIO D.   Agapito

A las   horas del   de

de mil novecientos

170

ro ___ 12 ___

REGISTRO CIVIL DE _Huelva_

DATOS DE IDENTIDAD DEL DIFUNTO: _varón_

Nombre `T[H][O][M][A][S]    R`

Primer apellido `D[I][E][T][Z]`

Segundo apellido `[                    ]`

hijo de ██████████ y de ██████████

Estado _____ nacionalidad _USA_

Nacido el día _dieciocho_ de _junio_

de _mil novecientos cuarenta y seis_

en _MILWAUKEE, WISCONSIN_

Inscrito al tomo ____ ████████████████

Domicilio último ████████████████

████████

DEFUNCION: Hora _____ día _veintidos_

de _agosto_ de _mil novecientos setenta y tres_

Lugar _Termino municipal de Huelva (Mazagatos)_

Causa _accidente del avión C-141 de los E.A. Norteamericanos_

El enterramiento será en _Estado Unidos de America_

DECLARACION DE D. _Orden del Sr. Comandante Juez Instructor_

En su calidad de _Juez al tenorial 1196/73_

Domicilio _____

Comprobación: Médico D. _____

Colegiado núm. _____ número del parte

OTROS TITULOS O DATOS

ENCARGADO D. _Gonzalo ___ Lopez_

SECRETARIO D. _Agapito ___ _

A las _____ horas del _____ de _octubre_

de _mil novecientos setenta y tres_

L 003885 P 014

Número 14

REGISTRO CIVIL DE *Huesca*

DATOS DE IDENTIDAD DEL DIFUNTO: varón

Nombre MIRIAM W

Primer apellido RUBIN

Segundo apellido

hijo de ▮▮▮▮ y de ▮▮▮▮

Estado ▮▮▮ nacionalidad USA

Nacido el día *veintidós* de *noviembre*
de *mil novecientos cuarenta, once*
en *NEW YORK STE., New York*

Inscrito al tomo ▮▮▮
Domicilio último ▮▮▮▮▮▮▮

DEFUNCION: Hora ____ día *veinte de*
de *abril* de *mil novecientos setenta y tres*
Lugar *Dirección Provincial de ____ (barcelona jam)*
Causa *accidente del ____ Civil de los E. U. de América*
El enterramiento será en *Estados Unidos de América*

DECLARACION DE D. *____ del ____*
de la Embajada de ____ de ____
En su calidad de *____ 138/73 - Fecha 27. 9. 1773*
Domicilio
Comprobación: Médico D.
Colegiado núm. ____ número del parte
OTROS TITULOS O DATOS

ENCARGADO D. *____*
SECRETARIO D. *____*
A las *____* horas del *____* de *____*
de *mil novecientos ____*

(left margin, rotated)
REGISTRO CIVIL DE HUESCA (Guardería)
Certifico que la presente certificación literal, expedida
con la autorización prevista en el artículo 23 del Reglamento
del Registro Civil, contiene la reproducción íntegra del asiento
correspondiente obrante en el tomo 12
de la Sección 3ª de este Registro Civil.
La Secretaria Doña MARIA DELA ox DE DIEGO PRIETO
Huesca a __ de __ de 2006

172

REGISTRO CIVIL DE

DATOS DE IDENTIDAD DEL DIFUNTO:

Nombre ▮▮▮▮▮▮

Primer apellido ▮▮▮▮▮

Segundo apellido

hijo de _____ y de ████████

Estado _____ nacionalidad _____

Nacido el día _____ de _____

de _____

en _____

Inscrito al tomo _____

Domicilio último ████████████████████████

████████████████

DEFUNCION: Hora _____ día _____

de _____ de _____

Lugar _____

Causa _____

El enterramiento será en _____

DECLARACION DE D. _____

_____

En su calidad de _____

Domicilio

Comprobación: Médico D.

Colegiado núm. _____ número del parte ____

OTROS TITULOS O DATOS

ENCARGADO D. _____

SECRETARIO D. _____

A las _____ horas del _____ de _____

de _____

173

L 003885 P 016

Número _15_

REGISTRO CIVIL DE _Hueva_

DATOS DE IDENTIDAD DEL DIFUNTO: _varón_

Nombre C L E N T O N G

Primer apellido C O B A I N

Segundo apellido [ ]

hija de _—_ y de ▮

Estado _____ nacionalidad _U.S.A_

Nacido el día _veintiseis_ de _agosto_

de _mil novecientos sesenta y siete_

en _SEATTLE, WASHINGTON_

Inscrito al tomo _____

Domicilio último ▮

DEFUNCION: Hora _____ día _cinco de_

de _agosto_ de _mil novecientos noventa y_

Lugar _término municipal de Hueva, Guadalajara_

Causa _____

El enterramiento será en _Estados Unidos de America_

DECLARACION DE D. _____

En su calidad de _____

Domicilio _____

Comprobación: Médico D.

Colegiado núm. _____ número del parte

OTROS TITULOS O DATOS

ENCARGADO D. _____

SECRETARIO D. _____

A las _____ horas del _____

de _mil novecientos noventa y_

REGISTRO CIVIL DE _Huelva_

DATOS DE IDENTIDAD DEL DIFUNTO:

Nombre EDWARD R

Primer apellido PEPRIESE

Segundo apellido

hijo de _____ y de ▊▊▊▊

Estado _____ nacionalidad USA

Nacido el dia _treinta_ de _julio_

de _mil novecientos treinta y tres_

en GAYSVILLE, VERMONT

Inscrito al tomo

Domicilio último ▊▊▊▊▊▊▊▊▊▊

▊▊▊▊▊

DEFUNCION: Hora _____ dia _veintidos_

de _agosto_ de _mil novecientos setenta y tres_

Lugar _termino municipal de Huelva (Encarnación)_

Causa _Accidente del avión C-121331 F.A. Norteamericana_

El enterramiento será en _Estados Unidos de América_

DECLARACION DE D. _Jefe del Dpto. documento que subscribe_
de la Base aérea de Morón del aire - Telefonía Prieto

En su calidad de _1318/73 - Fecha 27-9-1973_

Domicilio

Comprobación: Médico D.

Colegiado núm. _____ número del parte

OTROS TITULOS O DATOS

ENCARGADO D. _Gonzalo Sierra López_

SECRETARIO D. _Ezequiel Romero Jiménez_

A las _____ horas del _primero de octubre_

de _mil novecientos setenta y tres._

REGISTRO CIVIL DE _puebla_

Número _18_

DATOS DE IDENTIDAD DEL DIFUNTO: _varon_

Nombre S|I|D|N|E|Y| |M|

Primer apellido H|I|L|L|S|M|A|N|

Segundo apellido |

hijo de _____ y de ▓▓▓▓

Estado _____ nacionalidad U S A.

Nacido el día _dieciunebre de mayo_ de _mil novecientos treinta y dos_

en S A N F O R D , F L O R I D A

Inscrito al tomo _____

Domicilio último ▓▓▓▓▓▓▓▓▓▓▓▓▓▓
▓▓▓▓▓▓

DEFUNCION: Hora _____ día _veintidos_ de _agosto_ de _mil novecientos setenta..._

Lugar _término municipal de Nueva, Guadiana_

Causa _accidente del avión..._

El enterramiento será en _Estados Unidos de America_

DECLARACION DE D. _____

En su calidad de _____ 1/06/79 — fecha 27 9 1979

Domicilio _____

Comprobación: Médico D. _____

Colegiado núm. _____ número del parte _____

OTROS TITULOS O DATOS _____

ENCARGADO D. _____

SECRETARIO D. _____

A las _____ horas del _____ de _____ de _mil novecientos setenta y ..._

176

L 003885 P 019

0 _____ 12

REGISTRO CIVIL DE *Huelva*

DATOS DE IDENTIDAD DEL DIFUNTO: varón

Nombre   S H A A S L

Primer apellido   K A T S E 7 o S

Segundo apellido

hijo de ▮▮▮▮▮   y de ▮▮▮▮▮

Estado _____ nacionalidad *USA*

Nacido el día *veintisiete* de *agosto*

de *mil novecientos cuarenta y tres*

en *PROVIDENCE, RHODE ISLAND*

Inscrito al tomo _____

Domicilio último ▮▮▮▮▮▮▮▮▮▮

DEFUNCION: Hora _____ día *veintidós*

de *agosto* de *mil novecientos setenta y tres*

Lugar *término municipal de Huelva (Guadalajara)*

Causa *accidente del avión C-141 de las F.A. Norteamericanas*

El enterramiento será en *Estados Unidos de América*

DECLARACION DE D. *Orden del Sr Comandante Jefe Instructor de la Base aérea de Torrejón de Ardoz - Diligencias Previas*

En su calidad de *1196/73 - fecha 27-7-1973*

Domicilio _____

Comprobación: Médico D. _____

Colegiado núm. _____ número del parte _____

OTROS TITULOS O DATOS

ENCARGADO D. *Emerato Pérez López*

SECRETARIO D. *Agapito Romero Martínez*

A las *nueve* horas del *quince* de *octubre*

de *mil novecientos setenta y tres*

177

L 003885 P 02(

Número 30

REGISTRO CIVIL DE Nueva

DATOS DE IDENTIDAD DEL DIFUNTO: varón

Nombre ROBERT L

Primer apellido AQUILOWAY

Segundo apellido

hijo de ████████ y de

Estado nacionalidad USA

Nacido el día catorce de noviembre

de mil novecientos cuarenta y un

en DETROIT, MICHIGAN

Inscrito al tomo

Domicilio último ████████████████

DEFUNCION: Hora día diecisiete

de agosto de mil novecientos setenta

Lugar término municipal de Nueva (Huesca)

Causa accidente del avión c ivi sobre b. rotura

El enterramiento será en Estados Unidos de América

DECLARACION DE D. según del h comandante jur. jud.

de la Seretaria de campan militar Diligencias

En su calidad de 7796/73 — Fecha 27 9 1973

Domicilio

Comprobación: Médico D.

Colegiado núm. número del parte

OTROS TITULOS O DATOS

ENCARGADO D. Consuelo Ruiz López

SECRETARIO D. Agapito Ruiz Santero,

A las siete horas del quince de julio

de mil novecientos setenta y tre

(firma)

178

REGISTRO CIVIL DE *Muerte*

DATOS DE IDENTIDAD DEL DIFUNTO:

Nombre MICHAEL L

Primer apellido HENDRIKS

Segundo apellido

hijo de ███████ y de ███████

Estado _____ nacionalidad USA

Nacido el día *dos* de *enero*
de *mil novecientos cuarenta y tres*
en *NEW ORLEANS, LOUISIANA*

Inscrito al tomo ███████

Domicilio último ████████████████████████
███████████

DEFUNCION: Hora _____ día *veintidós*
de *agosto* de *mil novecientos setenta y tres*
Lugar *termino municipal de Huelva (Cruce de la playa)*
Causa *Accidente del avión : 141 de las F.A. Norteamericanos*
El enterramiento será en *Estados Unidos de América*

DECLARACION DE D. *Orden del Sr Comandante por instrucción*
de la base aérea de virgen de aires. Diligencias Previas
En su calidad de *1196/73.- Fecha 27-9-1973*

Domicilio _____

Comprobación: Médico D. _____

Colegiado núm. _____ número del parte _____

OTROS TITULOS O DATOS _____

ENCARGADO D. *Gonzalo Pérez López*
SECRETARIO D. *Agapito Romero Martínez*
A las *nueve* horas del *quince* de *octubre*
de *mil novecientos setenta y tres*

Número _20_

REGISTRO CIVIL DE _Huelva_

DATOS DE IDENTIDAD DEL DIFUNTO: _varón_

Nombre C L I F F O R D E

Primer apellido B A R R O W

Segundo apellido

hijo de ▮▮▮▮▮ *y de* ▮▮▮▮▮

Estado _____ *nacionalidad* _USA_

Nacido el día _treinta y uno de_ _mayo_

de _mil novecientos cuarenta y_ _____

en MEMPHIS, TENNESSEE

Inscrito al tomo _____

Domicilio último ▮▮▮▮▮▮▮▮

DEFUNCIÓN: Hora _____ *día* _veintidós_

de _agosto_ *de* _mil novecientos setenta y_ _____

Lugar _término municipal de Huelva (Guadalajara)_

Causa _accidente del avión C-141 de las F.A. Norteamericana_

El enterramiento será en _Estados Unidos de América_

DECLARACIÓN DE D _____

En su calidad de _____

Domicilio _____

Comprobación: Médico D. _____

Colegiado núm. _____ *número del parte* ____

OTROS TITULOS O DATOS _____

ENCARGADO D. _Consuelo Cano López_

SECRETARIO D. _Agapito Romero Machuca_

A las _____ *horas del* _primero_ *de* _____

de mil novecientos setenta y tres

---

ro   23

REGISTRO CIVIL DE _Hueva_

DATOS DE IDENTIDAD DEL DIFUNTO: hembra

Nombre `J A N I C E S`

Primer apellido `B A R R O W`

Segundo apellido

hijo de ▮▮▮▮▮▮▮▮ y de ▮▮▮▮▮▮▮▮

Estado _casada_   nacionalidad _USA_

Nacido el día _veintiseis_ de _enero_

de _mil novecientos cuarenta y dos_

en _MEMPHIS, TENNESSEE_

Inscrito al tomo

Domicilio último ▮▮▮▮▮▮▮▮▮▮▮

DEFUNCION: Hora   día _veintidos_

de _Agosto_   de _mil novecientos setenta y tres_

Lugar _Termino municipal de Hueva (Guadalajara)_

Causa _Accidente del avion C141 de las F.A. Norteamericanas_

El enterramiento será en _Estados Unidos de América_

DECLARACION DE D. _Miguel de Losanchanto Teniente_
de la Base Aerea de Torrejon de Ardoz - Diligencias Breves
En su calidad de _1196173 - Fecha 27-9-1973_

Domicilio

Comprobación: Médico D.

Colegiado núm.   número del parte

OTROS TITULOS O DATOS _La defunta estaba casada con_
Clifford E. Barron

ENCARGADO D. _Gonzalo Perez Lopez_

SECRETARIO D. _Afapelo Ramos Martinez_

A las _nueve_ horas del _quince de octubre_

de _mil novecientos setenta y tres,_

181

Número 24

REGISTRO CIVIL DE *Huelva*

DATOS DE IDENTIDAD DEL DIFUNTO:

Nombre FRANK B

Primer apellido MASSEY

Segundo apellido

hijo de ▓▓▓▓ y de ▓▓▓▓

Estado nacionalidad USA

Nacido el día *veintidos* de *julio*
de *mil novecientos treinta y tres*
en SLATON, TEXAS

Inscrito al tomo

Domicilio último ▓▓▓▓

DEFUNCION: Hora día *veintidós*
de *agosto* de *mil novecientos setenta y ...*
Lugar *término municipal de Huelva* ...
Causa *accidente del avión C-141 de la F.A. Norteamericana*
El enterramiento será en *Estados Unidos de América*

DECLARACION DE D. ...
En su calidad de 1196/73 - Fecha 27- 7-1973

Domicilio

Comprobación: Médico D.

Colegiado núm. número del parte

OTROS TITULOS O DATOS

ENCARGADO D. *Gonzalo Pérez López*

SECRETARIO D. *Agapito Pérez ...*

A las *nueve* horas del *quince* de *octubre*
de *mil novecientos ...*

L 003885   P 025

REGISTRO CIVIL DE _Hueva_

DATOS DE IDENTIDAD DEL DIFUNTO: _hombre_

Nombre MONTREAL

Primer apellido MASSEY

Segundo apellido

hijo de ▮▮▮▮ y de ▮▮▮▮

Estado _casada_   nacionalidad _USA_

Nacido el día _diecirueve_ de _agosto_

de _mil novecientos quincéoho_

en _MINNESOTA_

Inscrito al tomo

Domicilio último ▮▮▮▮

DEFUNCION: Hora _ _ día _veintiocho_

de _agosto_ de _mil novecientos setenta y tres_

Lugar _terreno jurisdic. de Hueva (Guadalajara)_

Causa _accidente de avión C-141 de las F.A. norteamericanas_

El enterramiento será en _Estados Unidos de Norte América_

DECLARACION DE D. _Orden del Sr. Teniente Juez Instructor de la base aérea de Torrejón de Ardoz - Oficios recibidos_

En su calidad de _1496/73 - fecha 27-8-1973_

Domicilio

Comprobación: Médico D.

Colegiado núm.   número del parte

OTROS TITULOS O DATOS _la difunta estaba casada con su Frank B. Massey_

ENCARGADO D. _Gonzalo Cana Lopez_

SECRETARIO D. _Agapito Amado Martinez_

A las _once_ horas del _quince_ de _octubre_ de _mil novecientos setenta y tres_

183

L 003885   P 026

REGISTRO CIVIL DE _Huelva_

DATOS DE IDENTIDAD DEL DIFUNTO:

Nombre C H A R L E S E L

Primer apellido L O B B

Segundo apellido

hijo de ▮▮▮▮▮ y de ▮▮▮▮▮

Estado   nacionalidad _USA_

Nacido el día _veintisiete_ de _noviembre_

de _mil novecientos treinta y seis_

en _GARY INDIANA_

Inscrito al tomo

Domicilio último ▮▮▮▮▮▮▮▮▮

DEFUNCION: Hora   día _veintidós_

de _agosto_ de _mil novecientos setenta y_

Lugar _Término municipal de Huelva (Ayuntamiento_

Causa _Accidente del avión C-141 de la F.A. norteamericana_

El enterramiento será en _Estados Unidos de América_

DECLARACION DE D. _José del T. Guasuante..._

de la base General... comisión de actos... Diligencia...

En su calidad de _1198/73 - Fecha 21-9-1973_

Domicilio

Comprobación. Médico D.

Colegiado núm.   número del parte

OTROS TITULOS O DATOS

ENCARGADO D. _Gonzalo Paris López_

SECRETARIO D. _Segundo Romero Contreras_

a las _nueve_ horas del _quince de octu-_

de mil novecientos setenta y tres.

Huelva

L 003885   P 027

REGISTRO CIVIL DE *Huelva*

DATOS DE IDENTIDAD DEL DIFUNTO: hembra

Nombre `GEORGIA`

Primer apellido `LORD`

Segundo apellido `[            ]`

hijo de ██████████ y de ██████████

Estado *casada* nacionalidad *griega*

Nacido el día *veinte* de *mayo*

de *mil novecientos cincuenta y uno*

en *AGIA MARMARA, ATTICA, GRECIA*

Inscrito al tomo

Domicilio ultimo ████████████████████

DEFUNCION: Hora día *miércoles*

de *agosto* de *mil novecientos setenta y tres*

Lugar *término municipal de Huelva (Guadalajara)*

Causa *accidente del avión C-141 de los E.U. Norteamericanos*

El enterramiento será en *Estados Unidos de América*

DECLARACION DE D *oria del tte. Comandante Jose Contreras*
de la Base Aérea de Torrejon de Ardoz - Diligencias previas
En su calidad de *1196/73 - Fecha 27-9-1973*

Domicilio

Comprobación: Médico D.

Colegiado núm. número del parte

OTROS TITULOS O DATOS *la difunta era esposa de*
Charles E. Lord.

ENCARGADO D. *Gonzalo Pérez López*

SECRETARIO D. *Angela Romero Fuentes*

nueve horas del *quince de octubre*
de *mil novecientos setenta y tres*

185

Número   28

REGISTRO CIVIL DE _Nueva_

DATOS DE IDENTIDAD DEL DIFUNTO: _varón_

Nombre   H A R R Y   G

Primer apellido   C A N T O N

Segundo apellido

hijo de   ███████   y de   ███████

Estado   nacionalidad _USA_

Nacido el día _catorce_ de _agosto_

de _mil novecientos cuarenta y ocho_

en _EAST DERRY, NEW HAMPSHIRE_

Inscrito al tomo

Domicilio último   ███████████

DEFUNCION: Hora   día _veintidos_

de _agosto_ de _mil novecientos setenta y tres_

Lugar _término municipal de Nueva (Guadalajara_

Causa _accidente del avión C-141 de la F.A. norteamericana_

El enterramiento será en _Estados Unidos de América_

DECLARACION DE D. _orden del Sr. Comandante Jefe Cuartel_
de la base aérea de Torrejón de Ardoz - Diligencias Policía

En su calidad de _1196/73 - Fecha 27-9-1973_

Domicilio

Comprobación: Médico D.

Colegiada núm.   número del parte

OTROS TITULOS O DATOS

ENCARGADO D. _Gonzalo García López_

SECRETARIO D. _Afapito Ramero Martínez_

A las _nueve_ horas del _quince de octubre_

de _mil novecientos setenta y tres_

v _____ 22

REGISTRO CIVIL DE *Nueva*

DATOS DE IDENTIDAD DEL DIFUNTO: *Sarita*

Nombre *SHARA R*

Primer apellido *CANTOR*

Segundo apellido

hijo de ___ y de ___

Estado *casada*   nacionalidad *USA*

Nacido el dia *veintiuno* de *febrero*

de *mil novecientos cuarenta*

en *California*

Inscrito al tomo

Domicilio último ████████████

DEFUNCION: Hora _____ dia *veintiocho*

de *agosto* de *mil novecientos setenta y tres*

Lugar *Término municipal de Nueva (Guadalajara)*

Causa *Accidente del aero. C-141 de la F.A. Norteamericana*

El enterramiento será en *Estados Unidos de América*

DECLARACION DE D. *en virtud de lo ....*

de la ....

En su calidad de *Juez .... Fecha 27-9-1973*

Domicilio

Comprobación: Médico D.

Colegiado núm. _____ número del parte

OTROS TITULOS O DATOS *Esposa de Barry G. Cantor*

ENCARGADO D. *Gonzalo Pérez López*

SECRETARIO D. *Agapito Romero Martínez*

a las *nueve* horas del *quince* de *octubre*

de *mil novecientos setenta y tres*

187

L 003885 P 030

Número 30

REGISTRO CIVIL DE *Hueva*

DATOS DE IDENTIDAD DEL DIFUNTO:

Nombre *MADELEINE MARI*

Primer apellido *Oswald*

Segundo apellido

hijo de ▮ y de ▮

Estado   nacionalidad *USA*

Nacido el día *quince* de *mayo*

de *mil novecientos treinta y nueve*

en *Miami (Florida)*

Inscrito al tomo ▮

Domicilio último ▮

DEFUNCION: Hora   día *veintidos*

de *agosto* de *mil novecientos setenta y tres*

Lugar *Término municipal de Hueva (Venosa), en*

Causa *Accidente del avión C-141 de la U.A. norteamericana*

El enterramiento será en *Estados Unidos de América*

DECLARACION DE D.

de la Presidencia de corregir de ceses - Villanueva etc.

En su calidad de *1196-73 - Fecha 27 - 9 1973*

Domicilio

Comprobación: Médico D.

Colegiado núm.   número del parte

OTROS TITULOS O DATOS

ENCARGADO D. *Gonzalo Pérez López*

SECRETARIO D. *Agapito Rivera Martínez*

A las *nueve* horas del *quince* de *setiembre*

de *mil novecientos setenta y tres*

188

L   003885   P   031

REGISTRO CIVIL DE *Huelva*

DATOS DE IDENTIDAD DEL DIFUNTO: *varón*

Nombre `C A R L E S G`

Primer apellido `H Y A T T`

Segundo apellido

hijo de ███████████ y de

Estado _____ nacionalidad USA

Nacido el día *diecisiete* de *febrero*
de *mil novecientos treinta y cuatro*
en *Waterloo, New York*

Inscrito al tomo
Domicilio último ██████████ ████████████

DEFUNCION: Hora _____ día *veintiocho*
de *agosto* de *mil novecientos setenta y tres*
Lugar *término municipal de Huesa (Guadalajara)*
Causa *Accidente del avión C-141 de las F.A. norteamericanas*
El enterramiento será en *Estados Unidos de América*

DECLARACION DE D. *Diego del P. Comandante Juez Instructor*
de la Brigada Paracaidista Tomo, instador - Diligencias Previas
En su calidad de *1196/73 - Fecha 27.9.1973*

Domicilio
Comprobación: Médico D.
Colegiado núm. _____ número del parte
OTROS TITULOS O DATOS

ENCARGADO D. *Gonzalo Pérez Agores*
SECRETARIO D. *Agapito Ramero Martínez*
las *nueve* horas del *quince de octubre*
de *mil novecientos setenta y tres.*

189

L 003885   P 032

REGISTRO CIVIL DE _Huelva_

DATOS DE IDENTIDAD DEL DIFUNTO: _varón_

Nombre P R I M A L I A

Primer apellido M A C I A S

Segundo apellido

hijo de ███████ y de ███████

Estado _____ nacionalidad _U.S.A_

Nacido el día _diez_ de _mayo_

de _mil novecientos cincuenta y dos_

en _Bonne Terre, Missouri_

Inscrito al tomo _____

Domicilio última ███████

DEFUNCION: Hora _____ día _veintiocho_

de _agosto_ de _mil novecientos setenta y dos_

Lugar _término municipal de Huelva (carretera)_

Causa _accidente del avión C-111 de la E. S. American_

El enterramiento será en _Estados Unidos de América_

DECLARACION DE D. _el Sr. Comandante _____ instr._
de la Brigada de tráfico de autos - Diligencia Prev.
En su calidad de _1196173 - Folia 27 - 8 - 1972_

Domicilio _____

Comprobación: Médico D. _____

Colegiado núm. _____ número del parte _____

OTROS TITULOS O DATOS _____

ENCARGADO D. _Gonzalo Pérez López_

SECRETARIO D. _Agapito Romero_ _____

A las _nueve_ horas del _quince_ de _octubre_

de _mil novecientos setenta y ...._

190

0   33

REGISTRO CIVIL DE *Huelva*

DATOS DE IDENTIDAD DEL DIFUNTO: ~~~~~

Nombre `T E R E S A   A.`

Primer apellido `W I L C O X`

Segundo apellido

hijo de ▮▮▮▮▮ y de ▮▮▮▮▮

Estado _____ nacionalidad *U.S.A.*

Nacido el dia *cinco* de *mayo*
de *mil novecientos cincuenta y tres*
en *Westerly, Rhode Island*

Inscrito al tomo _____

Domicilio último ▮▮▮▮▮▮▮▮▮▮▮

DEFUNCION: Hora _____ dia *veintidos*
de *Agosto* de *mil novecientos setenta y tres*
Lugar *término municipal de Huelva (Guadalajara)*
Causa *Accidente del avión C-141 de las F.A. norteamericanas*
El enterramiento será en *Estados Unidos de América*

DECLARACION DE Diego del Sr. Comandante Jose Urbiarte
de la Cruz Asesor de Asuntos debidos - Diligencias Urgentes
En su calidad de *1196/73 - Fecha 27.9.1973*

Domicilio _____

Comprobación: Medico D. _____

Colegiado núm. _____ número del parte _____

OTROS TITULOS O DATOS

ENCARGADO D. *Gonzalo Pérez López*

SECRETARIO D. *J. Capit. Rivas Martinez*

A las *nueve* horas del *quince* de *octubre*
de *mil novecientos setenta y tres*

(Rúbrica)

L   003885   P   034

Número _34_

REGISTRO CIVIL DE _Hueva_

DATOS DE IDENTIDAD DEL DIFUNTO:

Nombre AUSTIEN A

Primer apellido BAUMAN

Segundo apellido

hijo de — y de —

Estado nacionalidad USA

Nacido el día _cuatro_ de _agosto_

de _mil novecientos diez_

en _PARIS. ARKANSAS_

Inscrito al tomo

Domicilio último ███████████

DEFUNCION: Hora día _veintidós_

de _agosto_ de _mil novecientos setenta y tres_

Lugar _término municipal de Hueva (Guadalajara)_

Causa _accidente del avión C-141 de las F.A. Norteamericanas_

El enterramiento será en _Estados Unidos de América_

DECLARACION DE D. _Origen del 2º Comandante Jefe Instructor_
de la Brigada de aviones de carbón - diligencia pre-
En su calidad de _vias 1196 73 - Folio 27-9-1973_

Domicilio

Comprobación: Médico D.

Colegiado núm. número del parte

OTROS TITULOS O DATOS

ENCARGADO D. _Gonzalo Pérez López_

SECRETARIO D. _Agapito Romero Martínez_

A las _once_ horas del _quince de octubre_

de _mil novecientos setenta y tres_

192

L 003885   P 035

REGISTRO CIVIL DE *Hueva*

DATOS DE IDENTIDAD DEL DIFUNTO:

Nombre `EDWARD M`

Primer apellido `FLAGGE`

Segundo apellido

hijo de _____ y de ▮▮▮▮▮

Estado _____ nacionalidad *U.S.A.*

Nacido el día *ocho* de *abril*

de *mil novecientos veintiocho*

en *CALIFORNIA*

Inscrito al tomo ▮▮▮▮▮▮▮▮▮▮

Domicilio último ▮▮▮▮▮▮▮▮▮▮

▮▮▮▮▮▮

DEFUNCION: Hora _____ día *veintidós*

de *agosto* de *mil novecientos setenta y tres*

Lugar *Término Municipal de Hueva (Guadalajara)*

Causa *Accidente de avión a vía de la F.A. Norteamericana*

El enterramiento será en *Estados Unidos de América*

DECLARACION DE D. *Mandto. Comandante, Juez Instructor*
de la Base Aérea de Torrejón de Ardón - Diligencias Previas

En su calidad de *1170/73 - Fecha 27-9-1973*

Domicilio

Comprobación: Médico D.

Colegiado núm. _____ número del parte

OTROS TITULOS O DATOS

ENCARGADO D. *Gonzalo Ruiz López*

SECRETARIO D. *Angel Ramos Gutiérrez*

A las *nueve* horas del *quince* de *octubre*

de *mil novecientos setenta y tres*

(firma)

(texto lateral vertical izquierdo):
REGISTRO CIVIL DE HUEVA (Guadalajara)
Certifico que la presente certificación literal, expedida con la autorización prevista en el artículo 28 del Reglamento del Registro Civil, concuerda a reproducción íntegra del asiento correspondiente obrante en el tomo ___, de la Sección 3ª de este Registro Civil.
Hueva, a ___ de ___ de ___
EL SECRETARIO: Doña MARIA DE LA LUZ DE DIEGO PRIETO

35
193

THE STORY OF THIS BOOK ENDS HERE,

BUT THE INVESTIGATION WILL CONTINUE.

BIBLIOGRAPHY

THE AIRCRAFT

HANSEN PAUL M.: "C-141 LIFETIME MISHAP SUMMARY" 2013

LAUNIUS ROGER D., Airpower Journal Fall 1991: "A Revolution in Air Transport Acquiring the C-141 Starlifter".

Flight International 11 Junio 1964: "Visit to Georgia".

http://5.hueva.net/index.php/sucesos/accidente-aereo

http://www.c141flyingsquadrons.com/c-141-aircraft

http://www.c141heaven.info/index.php

https://en.wikipedia.org/wiki/JP-4_(fuel)

http://desarrolloydefensa.blogspot.com.es/2012/03/resena-de-aeronaves-de-transporte.html

http://amcmuseum.org/at-the-museum/aircraft/c-141a-starlifter/#comment-2940

http://www.gonavy.jp/bbs2-c141.html

FLIGHT ROUTE

Interview with William Haskel (Bill) Ray by Gustavo Doménech

Oficial USAF investigation report

THE ACCIDENT AUGUST 28 1973

Interview with William Haskel (Bill) Ray by Gustavo Doménech

Interview with Antonio Beas by Gustavo Doménech

Interview with Víctor Martínez Viana by Gustavo Doménech

Interview with Jesus Ramos by Gustavo Doménech

Interview with Steven Cansler by Gustavo Doménech

Technical assistance for aviation concepts by Paul Hansen

Oficial USAF investigation report

DISASTER RECOVERY

Interview with William Haskel (Bill) Ray by Gustavo Doménech

Interview with Antonio Beas by Gustavo Doménech

Interview with Víctor Martínez Viana by Gustavo Doménech

Interview with Jesus Ramos by Gustavo Doménech

Interview with Steven Cansler by Gustavo Doménech

Oficial USAF investigation report

CAUSES OF THE ACCIDENT

HANSEN PAUL M.: "C-141 LIFETIME MISHAP SUMMARY" 2013

MAC FLYER Magazine 1974. The final error.

Oficial USAF investigation report

https://www.aopa.org/training-and-safety/

http://c141heaven.info/dotcom/66/pic 66 7947.php

MEMORIAL CEREMONIES

Interview with Víctor Martínez Viana by Gustavo Doménech

"Trenton Times" September 5, 1973

http://www.tbmcguirefoundation.org/Dedication_11_2008.htm

http://www.jointbasemdl.af.mil/news/story.asp?id=123123697

http://c141heaven.info/dotcom/66/pic_66_7947.php

ANTONIO BEAS

Interview with Antonio Beas by Gustavo Doménech

VÍCTOR MARTÍNEZ VIANA

Interview with Víctor Martínez Viana by Gustavo Doménech

WILLIAM H. RAY

Interview with William Haskel (Bill) Ray by Gustavo Doménech

HUEVA (SPAIN)

FERNANDEZ IZQUIERDO, FRANCISCO: "La Villa de Hueva en su Historia". Ayuntamiento de Hueva (Guadalajara) 2003.

http://5.hueva.net/index.php/monu/iglesia

http://5.hueva.net/index.php/monu/picota

http://5.hueva.net/index.php/ayuntamiento-9

http://www.clubrural.com/que-ver/guadalajara/hueva

http://appfadeta.com/village/hueva/

http://appfadeta.com/poi/iglesia-de-nuestra-senora-de-la-zarza-hueva/

http://appfadeta.com/poi/casa-palacio-de-los-condes-de-zanini-hueva/

http://appfadeta.com/poi/picota-hueva/

http://www.escapadarural.com/que-hacer/hueva

NEWSPAPERS

Víctor Martínez Viana archive

Zayda Beas archive

"Desert Sun" August 29, 1973

"Asbury Park" August 29, 1973

"New York Times" August 29 and 30, 1973

"Trenton Times" August 29, 30 and 31, 1973

"Chicago Tribune" August 30, 1973

"Detroit Free Press" August 30, 1973

"Decano de la tarde" August 29, 1973

"Ya" August 30, 1973

"ABC" August 30, 1973

"Nueva Alcarria" August 30, 1973. September 1 1973. August 30, 2013. September 18, 2015

"La Vanguardia Española" August 30, 1973

"Mediterráneo" August 30, 1973

"Flores y Abejas" September 4, 1973

"Trenton Times" September 2 and 5, 1973

"La Actualidad Española" September 6, 1973

"The Leader" September 6, 1973

BOOK COVER

Courtesy of Rubén Puig, puigcop@hotmail.com

CPSIA information can be obtained
at www.ICGtesting.com
Printed in the USA
BVHW042001120721
611758BV00012B/504